Vintage Crochet Hats and Accessories

Vintage Crochet Hats and Accessories

23 Classic Hats, Shawls, and Bags

Kathryn Fulton

Photographs by Tiffany Blackstone

STACKPOLE
BOOKS

Published by
STACKPOLE BOOKS
5067 Ritter Road
Mechanicsburg, PA 17055
www.stackpolebooks.com

Printed in the United States of America

10 9 8 7 6 5 4 3 2 1

First edition

Cover design by Tessa J. Sweigert

Library of Congress Cataloging-in-Publication Data

Fulton, Kathryn, 1987-
  Vintage crochet hats and accessories : 23 classic hats, shawls, and bags /
Kathryn Fulton ; photographs by Tiffany Blackstone.
    pages cm
  Includes index.
  ISBN 978-0-8117-1447-1
  1. Crocheting—Patterns. I. Title.
  TT825.F844 2014
  746.43'4041—dc23
                        2014019845

Contents

Introduction

Everything old is new again. That's what they say—and it's certainly true in the world of fashion. Hemlines and necklines go up and down and then back up again, colors fall out of favor only to be rediscovered half a generation later, and the styles that once filled our grandparents' closets (and later, cedar chests and attic storage) are now back out on the streets and "hip" again.

Vintage fashions have seen a strong resurgence in recent days. Hipsters have repopularized the bow tie and the floral-print dress. Felt cloches and pin-striped fedoras fill the hat sections of department stores. Thrift shops see "ugly Christmas sweaters" flying off their shelves. We are rediscovering the playful fashions of the '20s, the cute practicality of the '50s, the bold colors of the '70s and '80s.

On top of that, the contemporary desire to "go green"—to make sustainable choices that minimize our impact on our planet's environment and reduce waste—plays into the popularity of vintage styles. Why buy cheap new clothes when our attics and second-hand shops are full of treasures? Or when we can make our own clothes and accessories, following in the footsteps of the women and men who carefully hand-crafted these vintage garments the first time around? Pouring time and effort into creating a handmade hat, shawl, or bag adds value to the item and ensures that it will not find its way into a landfill after just a few short months.

This book gives you what you need to do just that, with 23 classic patterns for hats, handbags, shawls, scarves, and other accessories, dating from the 1910s to the early 1960s. All the patterns have been carefully checked and edited where the original pattern was awkward or unclear, and the materials lists have been updated with modern yarn and hook information. You get the classic styles of the past without the hassle and guesswork of trying to interpet a decades-old pattern.

Re-create these fashions of the past and celebrate the old becoming new again!

Geometric Beanie

This classic beanie is made from basic stitches—double crochets, single crochets, and chains—put together in creative combinations to work a pattern of squares and triangles into the fabric, dressing up the simple shape. You get the visual interest of a subtle colorwork pattern without multiple strands of yarn to juggle.

YARN
Caron Simply Soft (100% acrylic; 315 yd./288 m; 6 oz./170 g), 1 skein in Pagoda

HOOK
U.S. size C-2 (2.75 mm) crochet hook or size needed to obtain gauge

NOTIONS
Yarn needle

FINISHED MEASUREMENTS
Circumference: 21 in. (53 cm)

GAUGE
19 sts in dc = 4 in. (10 cm)

PATTERN

Ch 5; join with a sl st to form a ring.

Round 1: Ch 1, work 8 sc in ring; join with a sl st in beg ch.

Round 2: Ch 3 (counts as 1 dc here and throughout), dc in same st as joining; 2 dc in next st and in each st around; join with a sl st in top ch of beg ch-3. (16 dc)

Round 3: Ch 3, dc in same st, *dc in next st, 2 dc in next st; rep from * to last st, dc in last st; join with a sl st in top of beg ch-3. (24 dc)

Round 4: Ch 4, *sk 1 st, sc in next st, ch 3; rep from * around; join with a sl st in 1st ch of beg ch-4.

Round 5: Ch 3, 3 dc in same ch-sp; work 4 dc in next ch-sp and in each ch-sp around; join with a sl st in top of beg ch-3.

Round 6: Repeat Round 4.

Round 7: Ch 3, 2 dc in same ch-sp; work 3 dc in next ch-sp and in each ch-sp around; join with a sl st in top of beg ch-3.

Round 8: Repeat Round 4.

Round 9: Repeat Round 7.

Round 10: Ch 4, *sk next 2 sts, sc in next st, ch 3; rep from * around; join with a sl st in 1st ch of beg ch-4.

Round 11: Repeat Round 7.

Rounds 12–15: Repeat Rounds 10–11.

Round 16: Ch 3, dc in next 4 sts, *ch 2, sk 1 st, 11 dc; rep from * around, ending last rep with 6 dc; join with a sl st in top of beg ch-3.

Round 17: Ch 3, dc in next 3 sts, *ch 2, dc in next ch-sp, ch 2, sk 1 st, 9 dc; rep from * around, ending last rep with 5 dc; join with a sl st in top of beg ch-3.

Round 18: Ch 3, dc in next 2 sts, *ch 2, [dc in next ch-sp, ch 2] twice, sk 1 st, 7 dc; rep from * around, ending last rep with 4 dc; join with a sl st in top of beg ch-3.

Round 19: Ch 3, dc in next st, *ch 2, [dc in next ch-sp, ch 2] 3 times, sk 1 st, 5 dc; rep from * around, ending last rep with 3 dc; join with a sl st in top of beg ch-3.

Round 20: Ch 3, *ch 2, [dc in next ch-sp, ch 2] 4 times, sk 1 st, 3 dc; rep from * around, ending last rep with 2 dc; join with a sl st in top of beg ch-3.

Round 21: Ch 5, *dc in next ch-sp, ch 2; rep from *
   around; join with a sl st in 3rd ch of beg ch-5.
Round 22: Ch 3, work 1 dc in each dc and each ch-
   sp around; join with a sl st in top of beg ch-3.
Round 23: Ch 3, dc in next 20 sts, *dc2tog, dc in
   next 21 sts; rep from * to last 2 sts, dc2tog; join
   with a sl st in top of beg ch-3.
Round 24: Ch 3, dc in next 10 sts, [dc2tog, dc in
   next 20 sts] 3 times, dc2tog, dc in next 9 sts; join
   with a sl st in top of beg ch-3.
Round 25: Ch 3, *sk next st, sc in next st, ch2; rep
   from * around; join with a sl st in 1st st of beg
   ch-3.

FINISHING
Weave in ends.

Candy Stripe Bag

Use this diagonally striped bag as a funky purse or to carry crochet projects. This project is a great place to play with color combinations and try out some of your favorites—use jewel tones, as shown here, or experiment with neon colors from the '80s!

4

Medium

YARN
Knit Picks Dishie (100% cotton;
190 yd./170 m; 3.5 oz./100 g),
2 skeins in Kenai, 1 skein in
Silver

HOOK
U.S. size H-8 (5.0 mm) crochet hook or size
needed to obtain gauge

FINISHED MEASUREMENTS
Base diameter: 6½ in. (17 cm); height: 9 in.
(23 cm)

GAUGE
5 sts and 5 rnds in sc = 1 in. (2.5 cm)

PATTERN

**This bag is worked in continuous rounds;
mark the end of each round but do not join
at the ends of rounds.**

BOTTOM
With A, ch 4; join with a sl st to form a ring.
Round 1: Work 6 sc in ring.
Round 2: Work 2 sc in each st around.
Round 3: *Sc in next st, 2 sc in next st; rep from *
around.
Round 4: *Sc in next 2 sts, 2 sc in next st; rep from *
around.
Round 5: *Sc in next 3 sts, 2 sc in next st; rep from *
around.
Round 6: *Sc in next 4 sts, 2 sc in next st; rep from *
around.
Round 7: *Sc in next 5 sts, 2 sc in next st; rep from *
around.
Round 8: *Sc in next 6 sts, 2 sc in next st; rep from *
around.
Round 9: *Sc in next 7 sts, 2 sc in next st; rep from *
around.

Round 10: *Sc in next 8 sts, 2 sc in next st; rep from
* around.
Round 11: *Sc in next 9 sts, 2 sc in next st; rep from
* around.
Round 12: *Sc in next 10 sts, 2 sc in next st; rep
from * around.
Round 13: *Sc in next 11 sts, 2 sc in next st; rep
from * around.
Round 14: *Sc in next 12 sts, 2 sc in next st; rep
from * around.
Round 15: *Sc in next 13 sts, 2 sc in next st; rep
from * around.
Round 16: *Sc in next 14 sts, 2 sc in next st; rep
from * 5 times, sc in last 15 sts.
Sl st in next st to even out end of round, then fasten
off.

VARIATION

With thick yarn and a tight gauge, as described here, the bottom piece will be sufficiently sturdy on its own. If you work with thinner yarn or at a looser gauge, you may want to make a second bottom piece for a sturdier bag. Work the sides directly onto one of the bottoms, as instructed here, and sew the other one onto it after the bag is finished. For even more stability, you can slide a piece of cardboard in between the two bottoms before you sew them together.

SIDES

Round 1: Continuing in A, sc in each st around.
Round 2: Sc tbl in each st around.
Join B.
Work *3 sc in B, 3 sc in A; rep from * around and continue past end of round without breaking the pattern. Continue to repeat these 6 sts until the piece measures 7 in. (18 cm) above Round 2.
Fasten off B. With A, repeat Round 1 three times.
Eyelet Round: Ch 3, *dc in next st, ch 1, sk next st; rep from * around; join with a sl st in top of beg ch-3.

Edging Round: Ch 1, *work [sc, 2 dc] in next ch-sp, sc in next ch-sp; rep from * around; join with a sl st in beg ch. Fasten off.

FINISHING

Weave in ends.

Cut 4 pieces of yarn about 80 in. (200 cm) long. Twist them together tightly, then double the twist back on itself to make a twisted cord. Tie each end firmly about an inch from the end and cut the folded end so that each end has a small tassel after the knot. Repeat to make a second twisted cord.

Thread one cord through the eyelet round and tie the ends of the cord together. Starting at the opposite side of the bag, thread the other cord through the same round, going under the stitches the first cord went over, and vice versa; tie the ends of the cord together.

Cherry Cloche

SKILL LEVEL

EASY

Remember the tune: "Can she make a cherry pie, Billy Boy, Billy Boy? Can she make a cherry pie, charming Billy?" Maybe a grand-mother, aunt, or mother sang that classic folk song to you; maybe you sang it to your own children or grandkids. You can remind today's "young things" of the old tune with this adorable hat trimmed with three perfect cherries.

YARN
Patons Classic Wool (100% pure new wool; 210 yd./192 m; 3.5 oz./100 g), 1 skein in Aran, scrap amounts in Leaf Green and Cherry

HOOK
U.S. size E-4 (3.5 mm) crochet hook or size needed to obtain gauge

NOTIONS
Yarn needle

FINISHED MEASUREMENTS
Circumference: 22 in. (56 cm)

GAUGE
8 sts and 9 rnds in sc = 2 in. (5 cm)

PATTERN

Ch 4; join with sl st to form a ring.
Round 1: Ch 1, 6 sc in ring; join with sl st in beg ch.
Round 2: Ch 1, 2 sc in same st and in each st around; join with a sl st in beg ch.
Round 3: Ch 1, *2 sc in next st, sc in next st; rep from * around; join with a sl st in beg ch.
Round 4: Ch 1, *sc in next 2 sts, 2 sc in next st; rep from * around; join with a sl st in beg ch.
Round 5: Ch 1, *sc in next st, 2 sc in next st, sc in next 2 sts; rep from * around; join with a sl st in beg ch.
Round 6: Ch 1, *sc in next 4 sts, 2 sc in next st; rep from * around; join with a sl st in beg ch.
Round 7: Ch 1, *sc in next st, 2 sc in next st, sc in next 4 sts; rep from * around; join with a sl st in beg ch.
Round 8: Ch 1, *sc in next 4 sts, 2 sc in next st, sc in next 2 sts; rep from * around; join with a sl st in beg ch.
Round 9: Ch 1, *2 sc in next st, sc in next 7 sts; rep from * around; join with a sl st in beg ch.
Round 10: Ch 1, *sc in next 7 sts, 2 sc in next st, sc in next st; rep from * around; join with a sl st in beg ch.

Round 11: Ch 1, *sc in next 3 sts, 2 sc in next st, sc in next 6 sts; rep from * around; join with a sl st in beg ch.
Round 12: Ch 1, *sc in next 10 sts, 2 sc in next st; rep from * around; join with a sl st in beg ch.
Round 13: Ch 1, *sc in next 6 sts, 2 sc in next st, sc in next 5 sts; rep from * around; join with a sl st in beg ch.
Round 14: Ch 1, *sc in next st, 2 sc in next st, sc in next 11 sts; rep from * around; join with a sl st in beg ch.
The piece should measure 6 inches in diameter at this point.
Round 15: Ch 1, sc in each st around; join with a sl st in beg ch—66 sts.
Repeat Round 15 until piece measures 5¾ inches from center to edge.

BRIM

Row 1: Ch 1, turn; *sc in next 4 sts, 2 sc in next st; rep from * to 3 1/2 inches from beginning of row, sl st in next st.

Row 2: Ch 1, turn; sl st in 2nd st from hook (skip the sl st), sc in each st across to last st, sl st in last st.

Rows 3–4: Repeat Row 2.

Row 5: Ch 1, turn; sk the sl st, sl st in next 2 sts, sc in each st across to last 2 sts, sl st in last 2 sts.

Row 6: Ch 1, turn; sk first 2 sts, sl st in next 2 sts, sc in each st across to last 2 sts, sl st in last 2 sts.

Rows 7–8: Repeat Row 6.

Row 9: Ch 1, turn; sk first 2 sts, sl st in next 4 sts, sc in each st across to last 4 sts, sl st in last 4 sts.

Row 10: Ch 1, turn; sk first 2 sts, sl st in next 6 sts, sc in each st across to last 4 sts, sl st in last 4 sts. Fasten off.

BAND

With contrasting color and starting in the back, work a row of sl st through the hat all the way around the first row of the brim. Join with a sl st and fasten off.

CHERRY (MAKE 3)

With red, ch 4. Join with a sl st to form a ring.

Round 1: Ch 1, 6 sc in ring, join with a sl st in beg ch.

Round 2: Ch 1, *sc in next st, 2 sc in next st; rep from * around; join with a sl st in beg ch.

Round 3: Ch 1, sc in each st around; join with a sl st in beg ch.

Rounds 4–5: Repeat round 3.

Stuff cherry with fiberfill and continue, working around the fiberfill to close the cherry around the stuffing.

Round 6: Ch 1, *sc in next st, sc2tog; rep from * around; join with a sl st in beg ch.

Repeat round 6 until 4 sts remain.

Last round: Sc4tog. Fasten off. Weave in ends.

Stems: With green, sl st in the top of a cherry. Crochet a chain about 5 inches long. Sl st in the top of another cherry. Fasten off.

Sl st in the top of the last cherry and crochet a chain about 1 inch long. Fasten off.

LEAF (MAKE 2)

With green, ch 12.

Row 1: Sl st in 2nd st from hook, then [sc, hdc, dc, 3 tr, dc, hdc, sc, sl st] along rest of chain. Work 2 more sl sts in last ch, then work the stitches in the brackets along the back of the chain. Fasten off.

FINISHING

Sew the leaves securely to the hat. Sew the end of the short stem and the middle of the long stem to the hat at the base of the leaves. Weave in all ends.

Stitched Scarf

Bundle up in this cozy, playful scarf that is easy and fun to make. It's crocheted horizontally, so the rows are *long*—but there's only 26 of them, and you'll be done before you know it. This scarf, made in school colors, is a great gift for graduates.

YARN
Bernat Vickie Howell Sheep(ish) (70% acrylic, 30% wool; 167 yd./153 m; 3 oz./85 g), 2 skeins in Teal(ish) (A), 1 skein in Chartreuse(ish) (B)

HOOK
U.S. size H-8 (5 mm) crochet hook or size needed to obtain gauge

FINISHED MEASUREMENTS
Length, not counting fringe: 56 in. (142 cm); width: 6½ in. (17 cm)

GAUGE
4 sts and 5 rows in (sc, ch1) pattern = 1 in. (2.5 cm)

PATTERN

With A, make a chain about the desired final scarf length (must be an even number of sts).

Row 1: Sc in second ch from hook, *ch 1, sk 1 ch, sc in next ch; rep from * across. Ch 1, turn.

Row 2: Sc in first st, sc in ch-sp, *ch 1, sk next st, sc in ch-sp; rep from * to last st, sc in last st. Ch 1, turn.

Row 3: Sc in first st, *ch 1, sk next st, sc in ch-sp; rep from * to last st, sc in last st. Ch 1, turn.

Row 4: Repeat Row 2.

Row 5: Repeat Row 3.

Row 6: Repeat Row 2.

Row 7: Ch 1, *ch 1, sk next st, hdc in ch-sp; rep from * to last st, hdc in last st. Ch 1, turn.

Rows 8–19: Repeat Rows 2–7 twice.

Rows 20–24: Repeat Rows 2–6.

Row 25: Repeat Row 3. Fasten off.

STRIPES

With B, work a ch slightly longer than the completed scarf. Fasten off. Make 3.

Weave the contrasting-color chains over and under the hdcs in Rows 7, 13, and 19, staggering the weaving of Row 13 so it is offset from the other two woven rows.

FRINGE

Cut strands of color A about 10 to 12 inches long by wrapping the yarn around a book or piece of cardboard and then cutting all the strands on one end. Take two strands and fold them in half, then pull the end of this loop through the space between the first two stitches of Row 1. Pull all four ends of the double loop through the loop and pull tight to attach the fringe. Repeat at

both ends of the scarf, at the end of every row
except Rows 7, 13, and 19.

Cut 12 pieces of color B the same length as the
other fringe strands. Attach the color B fringe in
pairs at the ends of the woven rows as for the
other fringe, bringing the fringe loop through
the end of the color B chains as well as around
the last stitch of the row to secure the woven
chains in the scarf.

FINISHING

Weave in all loose ends. If desired, trim the strands
of fringe to the same length.

Brewer's Stocking Cap

SKILL LEVEL

EASY

One of the oldest patterns in this book, this stocking cap is a style with a long history of keeping heads warm in the winter. It's easy to adjust this pattern if you want the floppy part of the hat to be shorter or longer; allow about 2½ in. (6 cm) for the decrease rounds (starting with Round 50) and add or omit repeats of Round 11 to get the length you want.

3
Light

YARN
KnitPicks Swish DK (100% superwash wool; 123 yd./ 112 m; 1.7 oz./50 g), 2 skeins in Lemongrass Heather

HOOK
U.S. size H-8 (5.0 mm) crochet hook or size needed to obtain gauge

NOTIONS
Yarn needle
Scrap piece of stiff cardboard

FINISHED MEASUREMENTS
Circumference (unstretched): 20 in. (51 cm)

GAUGE
17 sts in sc = 4 in. (10 cm)

PATTERN

Ch 77; join with a sl st in first ch.

Round 1: Ch 1, sc in same ch as joining and in each ch around; join with a sl st in beg ch.

Round 2: Ch 1, sc each st around; join with a sl st in beg ch.

Rounds 3–10: Repeat Round 2.

Round 11: Ch 1, sc tbl in each st around; join with a sl st in beg ch.

Rounds 12–49: Repeat Round 11.

Round 50: Ch 1, *sc tbl in next 9 sts, sc2tog tbl; rep from * around; join with a sl st in beg ch.

Round 51: Ch 1, *sc tbl in next 8 sts, sc2tog tbl; rep from * around; join with a sl st in beg ch.

Round 52: Ch1, *sc tbl in next 7 sts, sc2tog tbl; rep from * around; join with a sl st in beg ch.

Rounds 53–57: Repeat Round 11.

Round 58: Ch1, *sc tbl in next 6 sts, sc2tog tbl; rep from * around; join with a sl st in beg ch.

Round 59: Ch1, *sc tbl in next 5 sts, sc2tog tbl; rep from * around; join with a sl st in beg ch.

Round 60: Ch1, *sc tbl in next 4 sts, sc2tog tbl; rep from * around; join with a sl st in beg ch.

Round 61: Ch1, *sc tbl in next 3 sts, sc2tog tbl; rep from * around; join with a sl st in beg ch.

Round 62: Ch1, *sc tbl in next 2 sts, sc2tog tbl; rep from * around; join with a sl st in beg ch.

Round 63: Ch1, *sc tbl in next st, sc2tog tbl; rep from * around; join with a sl st in beg ch.

Round 64: Ch1, sc2tog tbl around; join with a sl st in beg ch.

Fasten off.

FINISHING

With a yarn needle, run a strand of yarn through the tops of the remaining sts; gather top of hat, then fasten off.

Cut a piece of cardboard about 5 in. (13 cm) wide. Wrap the yarn around the cardboard about 20 times, then cut the wraps along one edge to get a bundle of strands all about 10 in. (25 cm) long. Tie the bundle off in the middle with another

piece of yarn, leaving the ends of this yarn long to use to attach the tassel to the hat. Fold the bundle in half and wrap another piece of yarn around the doubled strands about 1 in. (2.5 cm) from the tied end. Fasten off tightly. Trim the bottom end of the tassel so all the strands are the same length, if desired, then use the yarn at the top of the tassel to attach it securely to the top of the hat.

The Brewer's Cap in 1901

Lazy Daisy Bucket Hat and Bag

Here's a nice summery hat and tote bag set perfect for gardening, picnics, and afternoon strolls. The hat and bag are made with the same yarn, but different hooks—the hat needs to be crocheted more tightly, so it holds its shape, while the bag must be crocheted more loosely, for flexible fabric. Be sure to check your gauge separately for each project.

Medium

YARN
Caron Simply Soft (100% acrylic; 315 yd./288 m; 6 oz./ 170 g), 1 skein each in Persimmon (A) and Off-White (B)

HOOK
Hat: Steel hook size 0 (2.55 mm) or size needed to obtain gauge
Bag: U.S. size G-6 (4.0 mm) crochet hook or size needed to obtain gauge
U.S. size P (10 mm) crochet hook

NOTIONS
Yarn needle
Fabric for bag lining
Circle of cardboard 6 in. in diameter
Sewing needle and thread to match lining

FINISHED MEASUREMENTS
Hat: Circumference: 22 in. (56 cm)
Bag: Bottom diameter: 6 1/2 in. (17 cm); height: 12 in. (30 cm)

GAUGE
Hat: 1 motif = 1 1/4 in. (3.2 cm) in diameter
Bag: 1 motif = 1 1/2 in. (3.8 cm) on diagonal from corner to corner

HAT

CENTER MOTIF

With A, ch 5; join with a sl st to form a ring. Ch 3 (counts as first dc throughout pattern), 11 dc in ring; join with a sl st in top of beg ch-3. Fasten off.

MOTIF ROUND 1

Use B for entire round.

Motif 1: Ch 5; join with a sl st to form a ring. Ch 3, 4 dc in ring, sl st in any dc of Center Motif, 11 more dc in ring; join with a sl st in top of beg ch-3. Fasten off.

Motif 2: Ch 5; join with a sl st to form a ring. Ch 3, sl st in 9th dc of prev motif, 4 dc in ring, sk 1 dc on Center Motif, sl st in next dc of Center Motif, * 11 more dc in ring, sl st in top of beg ch-3. Fasten off.

Motifs 3–5: Work as for Motif 2.

Motif 6: Work as for Motif 2 to *. 4 dc in ring, sl st in 2nd dc of Motif 1, 7 more dc in ring, sl st in top of beg ch-3. Fasten off.

MOTIF ROUND 2

Use A for entire round.

Motif 1: Ch 5; join with a sl st to form a ring. Ch 3, 4 dc in ring, sl st in 14th dc of any motif of prev round, 11 more dc in ring; join with a sl st in top of beg ch-3. Fasten off.

Motif 2: Ch 5; join with a sl st to form a ring. Ch 3, sl st in 9th dc of prev motif, 4 dc in ring, sk 2 dc on

same motif of prev round, sl st in next dc of round 1 motif, 11 more dc in ring, sl st in top of beg ch-3. Fasten off.

Motif 3: Ch 5; join with a sl st to form a ring. Ch 3, sl st in 9th dc of prev motif, 4 dc in ring, sl st in 15th dc of next motif of prev round, 11 more dc in ring, sl st in top of beg ch-3. Fasten off.

Motifs 4–11: Repeat Motifs 2–3 around (attaching 2 motifs to each motif of Round 1).

Motif 12: Ch 5; join with a sl st to form a ring. Ch 3, sl st in 9th dc of prev motif, 4 dc in ring, sk 1 dc on round 1 motif below, sl st in next dc of round 1 motif, 4 dc in ring, sl st in 2nd dc of Motif 1, 7 dc in ring, sl st in top of beg ch-3. Fasten off.

MOTIF ROUND 3

Use B for entire round.

Motif 1: Ch 5; join with a sl st to form a ring. Ch 3, 4 dc in ring, sl st in 14th dc of any motif of prev round, 11 more dc in ring; join with a sl st in top of beg ch-3. Fasten off.

Motif 2: Work as for Motif 3 of Round 2.

Motif 3: Work as for Motif 2 of Round 2.

Motif 4: Ch 5; join with a sl st to form a ring. Ch 3, sl st in 9th dc of prev motif, 4 dc in ring, sl st in 14th dc of next motif of prev round, 11 more dc in ring, sl st in top of beg ch-3. Fasten off.

Motifs 5–17: Repeat Motifs 2–4 around, ending with Motif 2 (i.e., attach 2 motifs to next motif of prev round, attach 1 motif to next motif of prev round, and repeat around).

Motif 18: Work as for Motif 12 of Round 2.

MOTIF ROUND 4

Use A for entire round.

Motif 1: Work as for Motif 1 of Round 3.

Motifs 2–17: Work as for Motif 4 of Round 3 (attaching 1 motif to each motif of prev round).

Motif 18: Ch 5; join with a sl st to form a ring. Ch 3, sl st in 9th dc of prev motif, 4 dc in ring, sl st in 14th dc of next Round 3 motif, 4 dc in ring, sl st in 2nd dc of Motif 1, 7 dc in ring, sl st in top of beg ch-3. Fasten off.

MOTIF ROUND 5

With B, repeat Motif Round 4.

BRIM

Round 1: Join color B in 14th dc of any motif of Motif Round 5. Ch 1, sc in same st; *ch 6, sc in center dc of next motif; rep from * around, ending with ch 6, sl st in beg ch.

Round 2: Ch 1, *sc in next 3 sts, 2 sc in next st; rep from * to last 2 sts, sc in last 2 sts; join with a sl st in beg ch.

Fasten off color B and join color A.

Round 3: With color A, ch 1, sc in each st around, join with a sl st in beg ch.

Rounds 4–8: Repeat Round 3.

Round 9: Ch 1, *sc in next 9 sts, 2 sc in next st; rep from * to last 7 sts, sc in last 7 sts; join with a sl st in beg ch.

Rounds 10–13: Repeat Round 3.

Round 14: Ch 1, sc tbl in each st around; join with a sl st in beg ch.

Round 15: Ch 1, *sc in next 8 sts, sc2tog; rep from * to last 2 sts, sc in last 2 sts; join with a sl st in beg ch.

Round 16: Repeat Round 3.

Round 17: Ch 1, *sc in next 4 sts, sc2tog; rep from * to last 5 sts, sc in last 5 sts; join with a sl st in beg ch.

Rounds 18–24: Repeat Round 3.

FINISHING

Turn brim under and sew last round to first round on inside.

BAG

The base of this bag is worked in continuous rounds; mark the end of each round but do not join at the ends of rounds.

BASE

With color A, ch 4; join with a sl st to form a ring.

Round 1: 6 sc in ring. Place marker for end of round; do not join this or following rounds.

Round 2: Work 2 sc in each st.

Round 3: *Sc in next st, 2 sc in next st; rep from * around.

Round 4: *Sc in next 2 sts, 2 sc in next st; rep from * around.

Round 5: *Sc in next 3 sts, 2 sc in next st; rep from * around.

Round 6: *Sc in next 4 sts, 2 sc in next st; rep from * around.

Round 7: *Sc in next 5 sts, 2 sc in next st; rep from * around.

Round 8: *Sc in next 6 sts, 2 sc in next st; rep from * around.

Round 9: *Sc in next 7 sts, 2 sc in next st; rep from * around.

Round 10: *Sc in next 8 sts, 2 sc in next st; rep from * around.

Round 11: *Sc in next 9 sts, 2 sc in next st; rep from * around.

Round 12: *Sc in next 10 sts, 2 sc in next st; rep from * around.

Round 13: *Sc in next 11 sts, 2 sc in next st; rep from * around.

Round 14: *Sc in next 12 sts, 2 sc in next st; rep from * around.

Round 15: *Sc in next 13 sts, 2 sc in next st; rep from * around.

Round 16: Sc in each st around.

Round 17: Sc tbl in each st around.

Round 18: Repeat Round 16.

Sl st in next 2 sts to even out rounds; fasten off.

SIDES

Motif Round 1 (color B)

Motif 1: Ch 5; join with a sl st to form a ring. Ch 3, 4 dc in ring, join with sl st to any sc on last round of base, work 11 more dc in ring; join with a sl st in beg ch-3; fasten off.

Motif 2: Ch 5; join with a sl st to form a ring. Ch 3, join with sl st to 9th dc of prev motif, work 4 dc in ring, sk 5 sc on last row of base and sl st in next sc, work 11 more dc in ring; join with a sl st in beg ch-3; fasten off.

Motifs 3–17: Repeat Motif 2.

Motif 18: Ch 5; join with a sl st to form a ring. Ch 3, join with sl st to 9th dc of prev motif, work 4 dc in ring, sk 5 sc on last row of base and sl st in next sc, work 4 more dc in ring, sl st in beg ch-3 of Motif 1, work 7 more dc in ring; join with a sl st in beg ch-3; fasten off.

Motif Round 2 (color A)

Motif 1: Ch 5; join with a sl st to form a ring. Ch 3, 4 dc in ring, join with sl st to 13th dc of any motif of prev round, work 11 more dc in ring; join with a sl st in beg ch-3; fasten off.

Motif 2: Ch 5; join with a sl st to form a ring. Ch 3, join with sl st to 9th dc of prev motif, work 4 dc in ring, sl st in 13th dc of next motif of prev round, work 11 more dc in ring; join with a sl st in beg ch-3; fasten off.

Motifs 3–17: Repeat Motif 2.

Motif 18: Ch 5; join with a sl st to form a ring. Ch 3, join with sl st to 9th dc of prev motif, work 4 dc in ring, sl st in 13th dc of next motif of prev round, work 4 more dc in ring, sl st in beg ch-3 of first motif, work 4 more dc in ring; join with a sl st in beg ch-3; fasten off.

Motif Round 3

Repeat Motif Round 2 with color B.

Motif Round 4

Repeat Motif Round 2 with color A.

Motif Rounds 5–6

Repeat rounds 3–4.

EDGING

Round 1: Join color A in 13th dc of any motif of Motif Round 6. Ch 1, sc in same st as joining, *ch 5, sc in 13th dc of next motif; rep from * around, ch 5, join with a sl st in beg ch.

Round 2: Ch 1, sc in next st, *5 sc in next ch-5 sp, sc in next sc; rep from * around, ch 5, join with a sl st in beg ch.

Round 3: Ch 5, *sk 2 sc, dc in next sc, ch 2; rep from * around, join with a sl st in 3rd ch of beg ch-5.

Round 4: Ch 5, 2 tr in ch-2 sp, *tr in dc, 2 tr in ch-2 sp; rep from * around, join with a sl st in 5th ch of beg ch-5. Fasten off.

FINISHING

Cut a piece of cardboard about 6 inches in diameter to fit in the bottom of the bag. Cut two circles of lining material $1/4$ in. (0.6 cm) larger than cardboard piece on every side. Sew circles together with right sides facing with a $1/4$ in. (0.6 cm) seam allowance, leaving an opening large enough to insert the cardboard. Turn right side

out and slide cardboard inside; then sew opening closed with whipstitch.

Cut another piece of lining material about 21 by 10 in. (53 by 25 cm). Sew short sides together with right sides inside; turn piece right side out. Sew the bottom edge of this tube to the fabric casing of the cardboard piece. Turn under top edge and hem. Place the lining inside the crocheted bag and sew the top edge to Round 2 of the edging.

With size P hook and 5 strands of color A held together, make a chain about 36 in. (91 cm) long. Fasten off. Thread the chain through the ch-2 sps in Round 3 of the edging and knot the ends together.

Flapper Cloche

Here's a hat that just screams vintage: This simple cloche style is straight out of the Roaring Twenties. Trim it with a pin-backed feather embellishment, as shown here, with a wide ribbon in a contrasting color, or with a crocheted flower.

YARN
Knit Picks Wool of the Andes Sport (100% wool; 137 yd./ 125 m; 1.8 oz./50 g), 3 skeins Claret Heather

HOOK
U.S. size G-6 (4.25 mm) crochet hook or size needed to obtain gauge

NOTIONS
Feathers or other embellishments

FINISHED MEASUREMENTS
Circumference: 22 in. (56 cm)

GAUGE
6 sts and 6.5 rows in sc = 1 in. (2.5 cm)

PATTERN

Ch 4; join with a sl st to form a ring.

Round 1: Ch 1, 5 sc in ring; join with a sl st in beg ch.

Round 2: Ch 1, 2 sc in same st as joining and in each st around; join with a sl st in beg ch.

Round 3: Repeat Round 2.

Round 4: Ch 1, *sc in next 3 sts, 2 sc in next st; rep from * around; join with a sl st in beg ch.

Round 5: Ch 1, *sc in next 4 sts, 2 sc in next st; rep from * around; join with a sl st in beg ch.

Round 6: Ch 1, *sc in next 5 sts, 2 sc in next st; rep from * around; join with a sl st in beg ch.

Round 7: Ch 1, *sc in next 6 sts, 2 sc in next st; rep from * around; join with a sl st in beg ch.

Round 8: Ch 1, *sc in next 7 sts, 2 sc in next st; rep from * around; join with a sl st in beg ch.

Rounds 9–19: Continue in established pattern.

Round 20: Ch 1, sc in each st around; join with a sl st in beg ch.

Round 21: Ch 1, *sc in next 19 sts, 2 sc in next st; rep from * 4 more times; sc to end; join with a sl st in beg ch. (115 sts)

Round 22: Repeat Round 20.

Round 23: Ch 1, *sc in next 20 sts, 2 sc in next st; rep from * 4 more times; sc to end; join with a sl st in beg ch. (120 sts)

Rounds 24–34: Repeat Round 20.

Try hat on after Round 34 to check the fit. The length should be just about ¾ in. (1.9 cm) short of where you would like the brim to sit against your neck. Work more or fewer repeats of Round 20 accordingly to adjust if the length is off.

Fasten off.

BRIM

Count from the row end join in the back to find the exact center front of the hat. Mark the center stitch (there should be 59 sts on each side of the center stitch).

Left Side of Brim

Row 1: Skip first 9 sts on left side of center stitch and join yarn in 10th st. Sc in same st as joining and in next 41 sts. (42 sts) Fasten off.

Row 2: Join yarn in 4th st of prev row; sc in same st as joining and in next 35 sts. (36 sts) Fasten off.

Row 3: Join yarn in 4th st of prev row; sc in same st as joining and in next 29 sts. (30 sts) Fasten off.

Row 4: Join yarn in 3rd st of prev row; sc in same st as joining and in each st to last 2 sts. (26 sts) Fasten off.

Rows 5–10: Repeat Row 4.

Row 11: Join yarn in first sc of prev row. Sc2tog. Fasten off.

Right Side of Brim

Row 1: Counting from center back join from main part of hat, skip first 9 sts on right side of back center and join yarn in 10th st. Sc in same st as joining and in next 41 sts. (42 sts) Fasten off.

Rows 2–14: Repeat Rows 2–11 of left side of brim.

Back Brim

Row 1: Join yarn in the sc2tog of row 11 of the left side of the brim. Work 2 sc in same stitch as joining. Sc in every stitch around the back of the hat, ending with 2 sc in the sc2tog of row 11 of the right side of the brim. Fasten off.

Row 2: Join yarn in first st of prev row. Work 2 sc in first st, then sc in each st across until last st, 2 sc in last st. Fasten off.

Rows 3–4: Repeat Row 2.

Front Brim

Turn hat inside out and work the front from the wrong side.

Row 1: Join yarn in first st of gap in front of hat. Sc in same st as joining and in each st across. (19 sts) Fasten off.

Row 2: Join yarn at edge of gap. Sc in the 3 sts skipped at beginning of row 2 of left side, sc in next 19 sts, sc in 3 sts skipped at end of row 2 of right side. Fasten off.

Row 3: Join yarn at edge of gap. Sc in the 3 sts skipped at beginning of row 3 of left side, sc in next 25 sts, sc in 3 sts skipped at end of row 3 of right side. Fasten off.

Row 4: Join yarn at edge of gap. Sc in the 2 sts skipped at beginning of same row on left side, in each st of prev row across front, and in the 2 sts skipped at the end of same row on right side. Fasten off.

Row 5: Join yarn at edge of gap. Sc in the 2 sts skipped at beginning of same row on left side. Work 1 sc into sc now reached of prev row, sc in each st of prev row across front, 1 sc into sc now reached from prev row. Sc in the 2 sts skipped at the end of same row on right side. Fasten off.

Rows 6–10: Repeat Rows 4–5, ending with Row 4.

Row 11: Join yarn at first row of band across back of hat, work 1 sc in same row end as joining, 1 sc in each of next 2 row ends of back band, 1 sc in each sc of last row, and 1 sc in each of next 3 rows of back band; fasten off.

Row 12: Join yarn at last row of band across back of hat, work 1 sc in same row end as joining, 1 sc in each of next 2 row ends of back band, 1 sc in each sc of last row, and 1 sc in each of next 3 rows of back band; fasten off.

Row 13: Join yarn in first st of last row, sc in same st as joining and in every st around. Fasten off.

Rows 14–15: Repeat Row 13.

Row 16: Join yarn in 7th st of last row, sc in same st as joining and in each st to last 6 sts. Fasten off.

Row 17: Join yarn in 5th st of last row, sc in same st as joining and in each st to last 4 sts. Fasten off.

Row 18: Join yarn in 4th st of last row, sc in same st as joining and in each st to last 3 sts. Fasten off.

Row 19: Repeat Row 18.

Row 20: Join yarn in middle of back brim of hat, sc in same st as joining and in every st around entire hat. Join with a sl st in beg sc.

FINISHING

Weave in ends. Block hat. Turn up front brim and stitch lightly into place. Trim with a cluster of feathers or other embellishments.

The Flapper Cloche in 1930

Shell Shawl

It doesn't get more clas-sic than this triangular shawl with an easy pat-tern of double crochet shells. This project is very satisfying to make because you start with the longest row, with each subsequent row shorter than the last, making it feel like you're getting faster and faster the longer you work on it.

YARN
Caron Simply Soft Light
(100% acrylic; 330 yd./301 m;
3 oz./85 g), 4 skeins in Heavy
Cream

HOOK
U.S. size G-6 (4.0 mm) crochet hook or size
needed to obtain gauge

FINISHED MEASUREMENTS
Wingspan: 85 in. (216 cm); length at longest
point (center of triangle): 21 in. (53 cm)

GAUGE
Gauge is flexible for this project. Work a small
swatch before you start to make sure you
are happy with the drape of the fabric.

PATTERN

Ch 350.

Row 1: Sc in second ch from hook, *sk 2 chs, 5 dc in
next ch, sk 2 chs, sc in next ch; rep from * to
end—58 shells.

Row 2: Ch 1, turn; sk 1st sc, sl st in next 2 sts, sc in
next st, *sk next 2 sts, 5 dc in next st, sk next 2
sts, sc in next st; rep from * to end—57 shells.

Repeat row 2, having 1 fewer shell in each row, until
2 shells remain.

Last row: Ch 1, turn; sl st in first 2 dc of first shell, sc
in next st, sk 2 sts, 7 dc in next st, sk 2 sts, sc in
next st. Do not turn.

EDGING

Continuing from end of last row of body of shawl,
work *7 dc in end st of next row, 1 sc in end st of
next row; rep from * to corner; work 9 dc in

corner sc. Sk next 2 chs, **sc in next ch (above a
shell from Row 1), sk 2 chs, 7 dc in next ch
(above a sc from Row 1), sk 2 chs; rep from **
across, ending with 9 dc in corner sc. Work last
side same as first side, ending with a sl st in first
sl st of last row of body of shawl. Fasten off.

FINISHING

Weave in ends. Block.

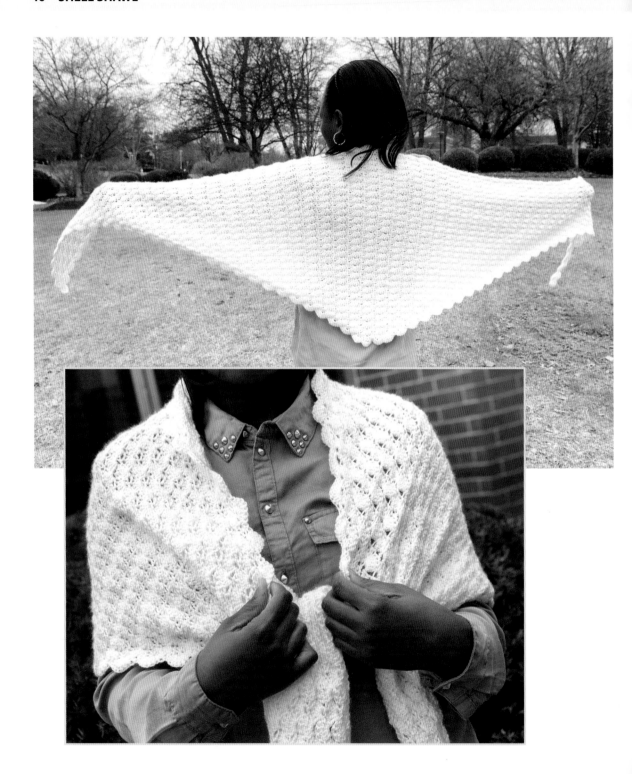

Button Cap

SKILL LEVEL

BEGINNER

This droll little hat is the perfect topper for a playful little girl. Let your little one join in the fun by picking out the buttons for her hat. If she has trouble picking just one style, no worries—using 6 different buttons just adds to the whimsical look!

YARN
Lion Brand Wool-Ease
(80% acrylic, 20% wool;
197 yd./180 m; 3 oz./85 g),
1 skein in Gold (#171)

HOOKS
U.S. size G-6 (4.25 mm) crochet hook or size
    needed to obtain gauge
U.S. size F-5 (3.75 mm) crochet hook

NOTIONS
6 buttons
Yarn needle

FINISHED MEASUREMENTS
Circumference at bottom brim: 14 in. (36 cm)

GAUGE
8 sts and 9 rnds in sc with larger hook = 2 in.
    (5 cm)

SPECIAL STITCHES
Reverse single crochet (rsc)

PATTERN

With larger hook, ch 3; join with a sl st to form a
    ring.
Round 1: Ch 1, 6 sc in ring; join with a sl st in beg
    ch.
Round 2: Ch 1, 2 sc in each st around; join with a sl
    st in beg ch.
Round 3: Ch 1, *sc in next st, 2 sc in next st; rep
    from * around; join with a sl st in beg ch.
Round 4: Ch 1, *2 sc in next st, sc in next 2 sts; rep
    from * around; join with a sl st in beg ch.
Round 5: Ch 1, *sc in next 2 sts, 2 sc in next st, sc in
    next st; rep from * around; join with a sl st in beg
    ch.
Round 6: Ch 1, *2 sc in next st, sc in next 4 sts; rep
    from * around; join with a sl st in beg ch.
Round 7: Ch 1, *sc in next 3 sts, 2 sc in next st, sc in
    next 2 sts; rep from * around; join with a sl st in
    beg ch.
Round 8: Ch 1, *2 sc in next st, sc in next 6 sts; rep
    from * around; join with a sl st in beg ch.

Round 9: Ch 1, *sc in next 4 sts, 2 sc in next st, sc in
    next 3 sts; rep from * around; join with a sl st in
    beg ch.
Round 10: Ch 1, *2 sc in next st, sc in next 8 sts; rep
    from * around; join with a sl st in beg ch.
Round 11: Ch 1, *sc in next 5 sts, 2 sc in next st, sc
    in next 4 sts; rep from * around; join with a sl st
    in beg ch.
Round 12: Ch 1, *2 sc in next st, sc in next 10 sts;
    rep from * around; join with a sl st in beg ch.
Round 13: Ch 1, *sc in next 6 sts, 2 sc in next st, sc
    in next 5 sts; rep from * around; join with a sl st
    in beg ch.

Round 14: Ch 1, *2 sc in next st, sc in next 12 sts; rep from * around; join with a sl st in beg ch.

Round 15: Ch 1, *sc in next 7 sts, 2 sc in next st, sc in next 6 sts; rep from * around; join with a sl st in beg ch.

Round 16: Ch 1, *2 sc in next st, sc in next 14 sts; rep from * around; join with a sl st in beg ch—96 sts.

Piece should measure 8 in. in diameter at this point.

Round 17: Ch 1, sc in each st around; join with a sl st in beg ch.

Rounds 18–24: Repeat Round 17.

Round 25: Ch 1, *sc2tog, sc in next 14 sts; rep from * around.

Round 26: Ch 1, *sc in next 7 sts, sc2tog, sc in next 6 sts; rep from * around.

Round 27: Ch 1, *sc2tog, sc in next 12 sts; rep from * around.

Round 28: Ch 1, *sc in next 6 sts, sc2tog, sc in next 5 sts; rep from * around.

Round 29: Ch 1, *sc2tog, sc in next 10 sts; rep from * around.

Round 30: Ch 1, *sc in next 5 sts, sc2tog, sc in next 4 sts; rep from * around.

Round 31: Ch 1, *sc2tog, sc in next 8 sts; rep from * around.

Round 32: Ch 1, *sc in next 4 sts, sc2tog, sc in next 3 sts; rep from * around.

Round 33: Ch 1, *sc2tog, sc in next 6 sts; rep from *
    around.
Round 34: Ch 1, *sc in next 3 sts, sc2tog, sc in next
    2 sts; rep from * around.
Round 35: Ch 1, *sc2tog, sc in next 4 sts; rep from *
    around.
The hat opening should be about 5½ in. in
    diameter at this point.
Change to smaller hook.
Rounds 36–41: Repeat Round 17.
Round 42: Ch 1; working from left to right, rsc in
    next st and in each st around; join with a sl st in
    beg ch. Fasten off.

LOOP
Ch 8.
Row 1: Sl st in each ch. Fasten off.
Sew to center of crown of beret.

FINISHING
Sew the buttons around the hat. Weave in ends.

Market Bag

SKILL LEVEL

EASY

Go green on grocery day by using a homemade, reusable bag for your purchases. This bag is made from sturdy cotton yarn and has an extra-thick handle so you can carry even the heaviest groceries in it.

YARN
Lily Sugar 'n Cream
(100% cotton; 200 yd./184 m;
4 oz./113 g), 2 skeins in Emerald
Isle (A), 1 skein in Indigo (B)

HOOK
U.S. size J-10 (6.0 mm) crochet hook or size
needed to obtain gauge

FINISHED MEASUREMENTS
Base diameter: 10 in. (25 cm); height, not
counting handles: 17 in. (43cm)

GAUGE
First 4 rounds = $2\frac{1}{2}$ in. (6.4 cm) in diameter

SPECIAL STITCH
Shell: Work 3 dc, ch 2, 3 dc in same st or ch-sp.

PATTERN

BASE
With A, ch 2.
Round 1: Work 7 sc in second ch from hook; join
with sl st in beg ch—7 sts.
Round 2: Ch 1, 2 sc in each st around; join with sl st
in beg ch—14 sts.
Round 3: Ch 1, *sc in next st, 2 sc in next st; join
with sl st in beg ch—21 sts.
Round 4: Ch 1, *sc in next 2 sts, 2 sc in next st; rep
from * around; join with sl st in beg ch—28 sts.
Round 5: Ch 1, *sc in next 3 sts, 2 sc in next st; rep
from * around; join with sl st in beg ch—35 sts.
Round 6: Ch 1, *sc in next 4 sts, 2 sc in next st; rep
from * around; join with sl st in beg ch—42 sts.
Round 7: Ch 1, *sc in next 5 sts, 2 sc in next st; rep
from * around; join with sl st in beg ch—49 sts.
Round 8: Ch 1, *sc in next 6 sts, 2 sc in next st; rep
from * around; join with sl st in beg ch—56 sts.
Round 9: Ch 1, *sc in next 7 sts, 2 sc in next st; rep
from * around; join with sl st in beg ch—63 sts.
Round 10: Ch 1, *sc in next 8 sts, 2 sc in next st; rep
from * around; join with sl st in beg ch—70 sts.

Round 11: Ch 1, *sc in next 9 sts, 2 sc in next st; rep
from * around; join with sl st in beg ch—77 sts.
Round 12: Ch 1, *sc in next 10 sts, 2 sc in next st;
rep from * around; join with sl st in beg ch—84
sts.
Round 13: Ch 1, *sc in next 11 sts, 2 sc in next st;
rep from * around; join with sl st in beg ch—91
sts.
Round 14: Ch 1, *sc in next 12 sts, 2 sc in next st;
rep from * around; join with sl st in beg ch—98
sts.
Round 15: Ch 1, *sc in next 13 sts, 2 sc in next st;
rep from * around; join with sl st in beg ch—105
sts.
Round 16: Ch 1, *sc in next 14 sts, 2 sc in next st;
rep from * around; join with sl st in beg ch—112
sts.

Round 17: Ch 1, BPsc in each st around.

Round 18: Ch 1, sc in each st around.

Round 19: Ch 1, *sc in next 20 sts, 2 sc in next st; rep from * around to last 12 sts, sc in last 12 sts—117 sts.

Rounds 20–24: Repeat Round 18.

Round 25: Sl st in next st, ch 3, 2 dc in next st, ch 2, 3 dc in same st, *sk next 3 sts, dc in next 2 sts, [ch 1, sk next st, dc in next st] twice, ch 1, sk next st, dc in next 2 sts, sk next 3 sts, **work shell in next st; rep from * around, ending last repeat at **. Join with sl st in 3rd ch of beg ch-3.

Round 26: Sl st in next 3 sts and in ch-sp, ch 3, 2 dc in same ch-2 sp, ch 2, 3 dc in same ch-2 sp, *sk next 3 sts, dc in next 2 sts, [ch 1, sk next ch, dc in next st] twice, ch 1, sk next ch, dc in next 2 sts, sk next 3 sts, **work shell in next ch-2 sp; rep from * around, ending last repeat at **. Join with sl st in 3rd ch of beg ch-3.

Rounds 27–42: Repeat Round 26.

Round 43: Ch 2, sc in next ch-2 sp, ch 2, *sk next 3 sts, dc in next 2 sts, [ch 1, sk next ch, dc in next st] twice, ch 1, sk next ch, dc in next 2 sts, sk next 3 sts, **ch 2, sc in next ch-2 sp, ch 2; rep from * around, ending last repeat at **. Join with sl st in beg ch.

Round 44: Ch 1, sc in each ch and st around, join with sl st in beg ch.

Round 45: Ch 1, sc in each st around, join with sl st in beg ch.

Rounds 46–47: Repeat Round 45.

Round 48: Ch 4 (counts as dc, ch 1), *sk next st, dc in next st, ch 1; rep from * around, join with sl st in 3rd ch of beg ch-3.

Round 49: Repeat Round 44.

Rounds 50–51: Repeat Round 45.

Fasten off.

DRAWSTRING

With B, ch 6. Join with a sl st to form a ring.

Round 1: Sc in each st around. Do not join at the end of the round.

Continue to work in continuous spiral rounds until drawstring measures about 50 in. (127 cm) or desired length.

Fasten off, leaving a long tail. Thread the drawstring through the spaces of Round 48 of the bag, going over and under every two double crochets. Use the tail to sew the end of the drawstring to the beginning.

Newsie Cap

SKILL LEVEL

INTERMEDIATE

Extra, extra—this newsie-style brimmed cap is not only stylish, it's also toasty warm. Add a splash of contrasting color with a simple crocheted flower and button, or leave it plain for a simpler look.

4

Medium

YARN
Lion Brand Heartland
(100% acrylic; 251 yd./230 m;
5 oz./142 g), 1 skein in Isle
Royale (MC), scrap amount in
Yellowstone (CC)

HOOK
U.S. size G-6 (4.0 mm) crochet hook or size
needed to obtain gauge

NOTIONS
Yarn needle
Sewing needle
Button, ⅝ in. (1.6 cm)

FINISHED MEASUREMENTS
Circumference at bottom of brim: 20 in.
(51 cm)

GAUGE
8 sts and 9 rnds in sc = 2 in. (5 cm)

PATTERN

BODY
With MC, ch 3; join with a sl st to form a ring.

> The hat is worked in a continous spiral up to
> the last few rounds. To help keep track of where each
> round begins and ends, mark the first stitch of
> each round with a stitch marker.

Round 1: 6 sc in ring.

Round 2: Beginning in first sc of Round 1 in order
to work in a continous spiral, work 2 sc in each st
around.

Round 3: *Sc in next st, 2 sc in next st; rep from *
around.

Round 4: *2 sc in next st, sc in next 2 sts; rep from *
around.

Round 5: *Sc in next 2 sts, 2 sc in next st, sc in next
st; rep from * around.

Round 6: *2 sc in next st, sc in next 4 sts; rep from *
around.

Round 7: *Sc in next 3 sts, 2 sc in next st, sc in next
2 sts; rep from * around.

Round 8: *2 sc in next st, sc in next 6 sts; rep from *
around.

Round 9: *Sc in next 4 sts, 2 sc in next st, sc in next
3 sts; rep from * around.

Round 10: *2 sc in next st, sc in next 8 sts; rep from
* around.

Round 11: *Sc in next 5 sts, 2 sc in next st, sc in
next 4 sts; rep from * around.

Round 12: *2 sc in next st, sc in next 10 sts; rep
from * around.

Round 13: *Sc in next 6 sts, 2 sc in next st, sc in
next 5 sts; rep from * around.

Round 14: *2 sc in next st, sc in next 12 sts; rep from * around.

Round 15: *Sc in next 7 sts, 2 sc in next st, sc in next 6 sts; rep from * around.

Round 16: *2 sc in next st, sc in next 14 sts; rep from * around.

Round 17: *Sc in next 8 sts, 2 sc in next st, sc in next 7 sts; rep from * around.

Round 18: *2 sc in next st, sc in next 16 sts; rep from * around.

Round 19: *Sc in next 9 sts, 2 sc in next st, sc in next 8 sts; rep from * around.

Rounds 20–25: Sc in each st around.

Round 26: Sc in each st around, decreasing 2 sts evenly over this round.

Round 27: *Sc in next 14 sts, sc2tog; rep from * around.

Round 28: *Sc in next 7 sts, sc2tog, sc in next 6 sts; rep from * around.

Round 29: *Sc in next 5 sts, sc2tog; rep from * around.

Round 30: *Sc in next 2 sts, sc2tog, sc in next 2 sts; rep from * around.

Round 31: *Sc in next 3 sts, sc2tog; sl st in first st of round to even out round.

Round 32: Ch 1, sc tfl in each st around; join with a sl st in beg ch.

Rounds 33–34: Ch 1, sc in each st around; join with a sl st in beg ch.

Fasten off.

BRIM

Row 1: Join yarn in 19th st of last round. Sc tfl in next st, *sc tfl in next 3 sts, 2 sc tfl in next st; rep from * 3 more times, sc tfl in next 4 sts; fasten off. (25 sts)

Row 2: Join yarn in 2nd st of prev row. Sc in each st across until one st remains; fasten off.

Rows 3–5: Repeat Row 2.

Row 6: Join yarn in 17th st of last round of body of hat. Sc in next 29 sts. Fasten off.

Row 7: Join yarn in 16th st of last round of body of hat. Sc in next 31 sts. Fasten off.

Row 8 (begin brim facing): Join yarn in same st as last row of brim. Sc tbl in next 31 sts; turn.

Row 9: Sl st in first 2 sts, sc in each st across to last 2 sts of prev row; turn (leaving last 2 sts of prev row unworked).

Rows 10–12: Repeat Row 9.

Row 13: Sl st in first 2 sts, sc in next 2 st, *sc2tog, sc in next 3 sts; rep from * 2 times; sl st in last 2 sts. Fasten off.

Row 14: Join yarn at edge of brim; working in unworked sts of Rows 8–13, sl st across bottom edge of brim facing. Fasten off.

FLOWER

Ch 5; join with sl st to form a ring.

Round 1: Ch 4, *hdc in ring, ch2; rep from * 5 more times; join with sl st in 3rd ch of beg ch-4.

Round 2: *Sc in next ch-sp, ch 4, sc in same ch-sp; rep from * around; join with a sl st in beg sc. Fasten off.

FINISHING

Turn facing portion of brim under and sew top edge of Row 14 to wrong side of brim. Weave in all ends; block hat if desired.

Sew a button to the brim of the hat. Slip the center of the flower around the button to attach it to the hat.

Sunbursts and Wildflowers Shawl

SKILL LEVEL

■■■■

EXPERIENCED

You'll be ready for summer weddings, picnics, and parties with this soft, light cotton shawl. In its original incarnation, this shawl was worked in a solid color. We've mixed it up with flowers in different shades of blue, but you could also do a rainbow version with flowers in every color.

YARN
Knit Picks Comfy (75% pima cotton, 25% acrylic; 218 yd./ 200 m; 1.8 oz./50 g), 3 skeins in Parchment (MC), 1 skein each in Planetarium (A), Marlin (B), and Sea Foam (C)

Super Fine

HOOK
U.S. size E-4 (3.5 mm) crochet hook or size needed to obtain gauge

FINISHED MEASUREMENTS
Width at top (longest) edge: 60 in. (152 cm); width at bottom edge: 32 in. (81 cm); length in center: 40 in. (102 cm)

GAUGE
Gauge is flexible for this project. Work a motif or two before you start to make sure you are happy with the drape of the fabric.

SPECIAL STITCHES
Picot: Ch 3, then sc in 3rd ch from hook.

PATTERN

FLOWER MOTIF
Ch 6, join with a sl st to form a ring.
Round 1: Ch 3, tr4tog through ring, ch 5, [tr5tog through ring, ch 5] 5 times, join with a sl st in first tr4tog. Fasten off if using a contrasting color; if using MC, continue.
Round 2 (first motif of strip only): Join MC in tr4tog of prev rnd. Sc in same st as joining, ch 5, sc in next ch-5 sp, ch 5, *sc in next tr5tog, ch 5, sc in next ch-5 sp, ch 5; rep from * around, join with sl st in beg sc.
Round 2 (all following motifs): If Round 1 was in a contrasting color, join MC in tr4tog of prev rnd. Sc in same st as joining, ch 2, sl st in last ch-5 sp of prev motif, ch 2, sc in next ch-5 sp of current motif, ch 2, sl st in next ch-5 sp of prev motif, ch 2, *sc in next tr5tog of current motif, ch 5, sc in next ch-5 sp, ch5; rep from * around, join with sl st in beg sc.
Fasten off.

FLOWER STRIPS
Make four strips of flower motifs using the colors indicated in the chart and joining each motif to the strip as you work Round 2. Strip 1 should have 15 flower motifs; Strip 3 should have 13; Strip 5 should have 11; and Strip 7 should have 9.

Outer Rounds
Round 1: Join MC to first motif of the strip, in the ch-5 sp five spaces before the join with motif 2. Sc in same ch-5 sp as joining. *[Ch 5, sc in next ch-5 sp] 4 times; ch 5, sc in sl st between motifs. Rep from * across to last motif; [ch 5, sc in next ch-5 sp of last motif] 10 times; ch 5, sc in sl st between first 2 motifs on 2nd side of piece. Work

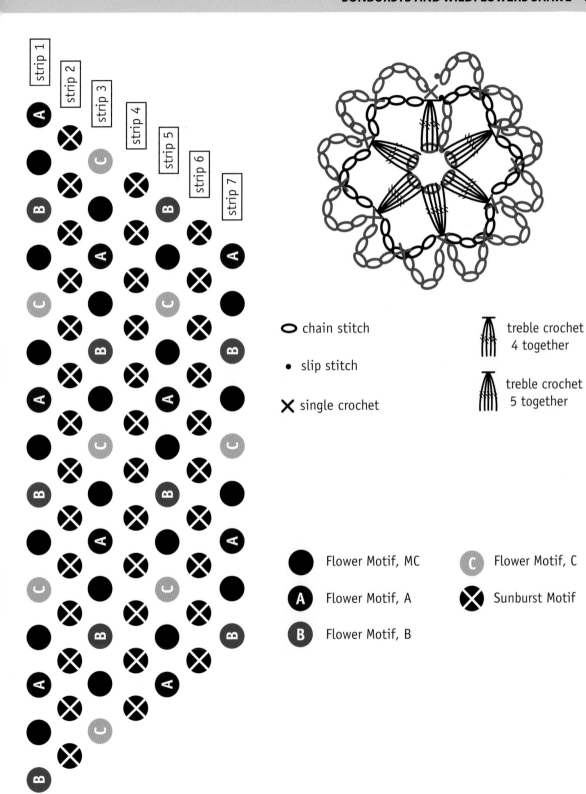

strip 1
strip 2
strip 3
strip 4
strip 5
strip 6
strip 7

chain stitch

• slip stitch

✕ single crochet

treble crochet
4 together

treble crochet
5 together

● Flower Motif, MC

Ⓐ Flower Motif, A

Ⓑ Flower Motif, B

Ⓒ Flower Motif, C

✕ Sunburst Motif

across 2nd side of piece as for 1st side, ending
with ch 2, dc in first sc of round.

Round 2: Sc in loop just formed, [ch 5, sc in next
ch-5 sp] twice; *ch 5, [tr, ch 3, tr, ch 3, tr] in next
ch-5 sp (shell formed), [ch 5, sc in next ch-5 sp]
twice, ch 1, sc in next ch-5 sp, ch 5, sc in next ch-
5 sp. Rep from * across 1st side, ending with [ch
5, sc in next ch-5 sp] 5 times instead of 2 after
last shell; shell in next ch-5 sp of last motif on
2nd side. Work across 2nd side of piece as for
1st side, ending with ch 2, dc in first sc of round.

Round 3: Sc in loop just formed, [ch 5, sc in next
sp] 7 times; *ch 2, sk next ch-sp, sc in next sp, [ch
5, sc in next sp] 5 times. Rep from * across 1st
side, ending with [ch 5, sc in next sp] 13 times;
ch 2, sc in next sp on 2nd side. Work across 2nd

side of piece as for 1st side, ending with ch 5, sl
st in first sc.

Fasten off.

Work the outer rounds on all the flower strips
before working the joining strips.

SUNBURST MOTIF

With MC, ch 6, join with a sl st to form a ring.

Round 1: Ch 9 (counts as tr, ch 5), [tr in ring, ch 5] 5 times, join with a sl st in 4th ch of beg ch-9.

Round 2 (first motif of strip only): Sc in same ch as joining, ch 5, sc in next ch-5 sp, ch 5, *sc in next tr, ch 5, sc in next ch-5 sp, ch 5; rep from * around, join with sl st in beg sc.

Round 2 (all following motifs): Sc in same ch as joining, ch 2, sl st in last ch-5 sp of prev motif, ch 2, sc in next ch-5 sp of current motif, ch 2, sl st in next ch-5 sp of prev motif, ch 2, *sc in next tr of current motif, ch 5, sc in next ch-5 sp, ch5; rep from * around, join with sl st in beg sc.

Fasten off.

SUNBURST STRIPS

Make 3 strips of sunburst motifs as indicated in the chart (Strip 2 has 14 motifs; Strip 4 has 12 motifs; Strip 6 has 10 motifs). Follow the instructions below to join the corresponding flower strips together.

Outer Rounds

Work Outer Rounds 1 and 2 as for the flower strips. Lay out the strip between the flower strips that come above and below it (the longer and shorter strips, respectively) and join it to the flower strips as you work Round 3.

Round 3: Sc in loop just formed, [ch 5, sc in next sp] twice, ch 2, sl st in center sp directly over center tr of shell on first motif of longer flower strip, *[ch 2, sc in next sp on sunburst strip, ch 2, sl st in next sp on flower strip] twice, ch 2, sk next ch-2 sp on flower strip, [sl st in next sp on flower strip, ch 2, sc in next sp on sunburst strip, ch 2] 3 times; ch 2, sk next ch-1 sp on sunburst strip, sc in next sp on sunburst strip, ch 2, sl st in same space on flower strip as prev sl st. Rep from * across until center sp of last motif on longer flower strip has been joined.

Then: ch 2, sc in next sp on sunburst strip, [ch 5, sc in next sp] 5 times, ch 2, sl st in the second ch-5 sp before the center sp directly over the center tr of shell on first motif of shorter flower strip. Continue across, joining shorter flower strip to sunburst strip in the same pattern as for the longer flower strip, ending in the ch-2 sp 2 spaces after the center sp of the last flower motif, then working ch 2, sc in next ch-5 sp of sunburst strip, ch 5, [sc in next sp, ch 5] to end of round, join with sl st in beginning ch.

EDGING

Top Edge: With right side of top (longest) edge facing, join B in the 4th ch-5 sp before the first ch-2 sp (top right corner loop), sc in same sp as joining. *[Ch 2, picot, ch 2, sc] twice in next sp, [ch 2, picot, ch 2, sc in next sp] twice, ch 2, dc in next ch-2 sp, picot, ch 2, sc in next space, [ch 2, picot, ch 2, sc in next sp] once. Rep from * across to sp 2 spaces after last ch-2 sp of top edge.

Turn Top Corner: *[Ch 2, picot, ch 2, sc] twice in next sp, [ch 2, picot, ch 2, sc in next sp] 3 times. Rep from * once more.

Side Edge: *Ch 2, dc in next sl st, picot, ch 2, sc in next sp; [ch 2, picot, ch 2, sc in next space] once, [ch 2, picot, ch 2, sc] twice in next sp; [ch 2, picot, ch 2, sc in next sp] twice. Rep from * across to end of edge.

Bottom Edge: Work same as Top Edge from * across to sp 2 spaces after last ch-2 sp of bottom edge.

Turn Bottom Corner: *[Ch 2, picot, ch 2, sc] twice in next sp, [ch 2, picot, ch 2, sc in next sp] twice. Rep from * once more.

Second Side Edge: Work same as the first side edge. At end of edge, ch 2, picot, ch 2, sc in next sp, ch 2, picot, ch 2 to reach end of round, then join with a sl st in beg sc.

Fasten off.

FINISHING

Weave in ends. Block shawl to even out the lace pattern, if desired.

The Sunbursts and Wildflowers Shawl in 1951

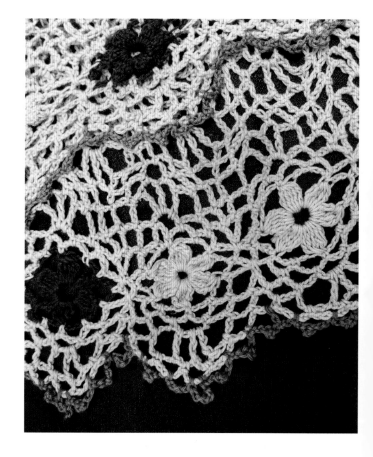

Santa Fe Belt

SKILL LEVEL

EASY

This geometric belt is quick and easy to make and works in any color scheme. The buttonholes are part of the stitch pattern for the whole belt, which means it's completely adjustable. Plan your foundation chain so it will be about the right length, but don't worry if it comes out a little longer than you intended.

3

Light

YARN
Knit Picks CotLin (70% tanguis cotton, 30% linen; 123 yd./ 112 m; 1.8 oz./50 g), 1 skein each in Coffee (A), Harbor (B), and Clementine (C)

HOOK
U.S. size G-6 (4.0 mm) crochet hook or size needed to obtain gauge

NOTIONS
2 buttons, 1 in. (2.5 cm) in diameter

FINISHED MEASUREMENT
Width: 3 in. (8 cm). Length is adjustable; sample shown measures 31 in. (79 cm) long.

GAUGE
4 sts and 3 rows in hdc = 1 in. (2.5 cm)

PATTERN

With A, ch 134 (or any multiple of 6 sts + 2 to measure a little longer than desired final length).

Row 1: Hdc in 3rd ch from hook and in each ch across. Break off A and join B. Turn.

Row 2: With B, ch 2. Hdc in 2nd st from hook and in next 3 sts, *ch 3, sk next 3 sts, hdc in next 3 sts; rep from * to end. Break off B and join A. Turn.

Row 3: With A, ch 2. Hdc in each st across. Break off A and join C. Turn.

Row 4: With C, ch 2. Hdc in 2nd st from hook and in next 6 sts, *ch 3, sk next 3 sts, hdc in next 3 sts; rep from * to last 3 sts, hdc in last 3 sts. Break off C and join A. Turn.

Row 5: Repeat Row 3.

Row 6: Repeat Row 2.

Row 7: Repeat Row 3.

Fasten off.

Edging Row: Join color A anywhere on edge of piece and work 1 row of sc around entire edge of belt (top, bottom, and sides), working 3 sc in each corner stitch.

Break off A and join C. With C, repeat Edging Row. Fasten off.

FINISHING
Sew the buttons to the end of the belt with more solid space before the holes.

Margaret Cloche

The textured pattern used in this cloche-style hat keeps the work interesting and gives a breathable fabric. It's the perfect accessory for those fall and spring days when the temperature is still unpredictable. You can also make a warmer version using bulky-weight yarn.

YARN
Knit Picks Comfy Worsted
(75% pima cotton, 25% acrylic;
109 yd./100 m; 1.7 oz./50 g),
2 skeins in Pomegranate

HOOK
U.S. size G-6 (4.25 mm) crochet hook or size
needed to obtain gauge

FINISHED MEASUREMENTS
Circumference: 22 in. (56 cm)

GAUGE
16 sts in sc = 4 in. (10 cm)

PATTERN

Ch 4, join with sl st to form a ring.

Round 1: Ch 1, 6 sc in ring; join with a sl st in beg ch.

Round 2: Ch 3, dc in same st as joining, ch 1, *2 dc in next sc, ch 1; rep from * around; join with a sl st in top of beg ch-3.

Round 3: Ch 3, *sc in next dc, ch 3; rep from * around; join with a sl st in 1st ch of beg ch-3— 12 ch-3 sps.

Round 4: Sl st into next ch-3 sp, ch 3, dc in same ch-3 space, ch 1, *2 dc in next ch-3 sp, ch 1; rep from * around; join with a sl st in 3rd ch of beg ch-3.

Round 5: *Ch 3, sc in next dc, ch 3, sk the ch-sp and next dc, sc in next dc, ch 3, sc in next dc; rep from * around; join with a sl st in 1st ch of beg ch-3— 18 ch-3 sps.

Round 6: Repeat Round 4.

Round 7: Sl st in next dc, ch 3, sk the ch-sp, sc in next dc, ch 3, sc in next dc, *ch 3, sk next ch-sp and dc, sc in next dc, ch 3, sc in next dc, ch 3**, sc

in next dc; rep from *, ending last rep at **; join with a sl st in beg sl st.

Round 8: Repeat round 4.

Round 9: *Ch 3, sk next dc and ch-sp, sc in next dc; rep from * around; join with a sl st in first ch of beg ch-3.

Rounds 10–15: Repeat Rounds 8–9.

Round 16: Sl st in ch-3 sp, ch 3, dc in same ch-3 sp, 2 dc in next ch-3 sp and in each ch-3 space around; join with a sl st in 3rd ch of beg ch-3.

Round 17: Ch 1, sc in same st as joining, sc in next dc, *2 sc in each of next 3 sts, sc in next st; rep from * around. Do not join.

Round 18: Sc in each sc around.

Rounds 19–23: Repeat Round 18.

Round 24: *Sc in next st, sc2tog 3 times; rep from *
around; at end sl st in next 2 sts to even out
brim.

FINISHING
Fold brim under and sew last round to first round
of brim.
Trim with a ribbon.

The Margaret Cloche in 1955

VARIATION
For a bigger, warmer hat,
try a bulky-weight yarn
and a larger hook. The hat
shown here was crocheted
with Knit Picks Billow yarn (a
bulky-weight cotton yarn)
and a size H-8 (5.0 mm)
hook, and measures 26 in.
(66 cm) around at the bottom edge.

Dignified Tam O'Shanter

Named after the hero of a Robert Burns poem of the same name, the tam o'shanter is a traditional Scottish hat that's been worn since the 1400s. Tam o'shanters are usually made from tartan wool fabric, but you can make a crocheted version that's just as warm.

YARN
Knit Picks Full Circle (100% wool; 220 yd./200 m; 3.5 oz./100 g), 2 skeins in Ponderosa

Medium

HOOK
U.S. size H-8 (5.0 mm) crochet hook or size needed to obtain gauge

NOTIONS
Small amount of scrap cardboard

FINISHED MEASUREMENTS
Circumference at brim: 21 in. (53 cm)

GAUGE
11 sts and 10 rnds in sc = 2 in. (5 cm)

PATTERN

Ch 4; join with a sl st to form a ring.

Round 1: Ch 1, 8 sc in ring; join with sl st in beg ch.

Round 2: Ch 1, 2 sc in each st around; join with a sl st in beg ch.

Round 3: Ch 1, *sc in next 2 sts, FPdc in next stitch; rep from * around; join with a sl st in beg ch.

Round 4: Ch 1, *sc in next 3 sts, FPdc in same st as last sc (FPdc from prev rnd); rep from * around; join with a sl st in beg ch.

Round 5: Ch 1, *sc in next 4 sts, FPdc in same st as last sc (FPdc from prev rnd); rep from * around; join with a sl st in beg ch.

Round 6: Ch 1, *sc in next 5 sts, FPdc in same st as last sc; rep from * around; join with a sl st in beg ch.

Round 7: Ch 1, *sc in next 6 sts, FPdc in same st as last sc; rep from * around; join with a sl st in beg ch.

Rounds 8–19: Continue in established pattern. Tam should measure approximately 11 in. (28 cm) across at end of Round 11.

Round 20: Ch 1, *sc in next 16 sts, sc2tog, FPdc in next st (FPdc from prev rnd); rep from * around; join with a sl st in beg ch.

Round 21: Ch 1, *sc in next 15 sts, sc2tog, FPdc in next st; rep from * around; join with a sl st in beg ch.

Round 22: Ch 1, *sc in next 14 sts, sc2tog, FPdc in next st; rep from * around; join with a sl st in beg ch.

Rounds 23–29: Continue in established pattern.

BRIM

Round 30: Ch 1, *sc in next 8 sts, sk next st; rep from * around; join with a sl st in beg ch.

Round 31: Ch 1, sc in next st and in each st around.

Rounds 32–37: Repeat Round 31.

Fasten off.

The Dignified Tam O'Shanter in 1901

POM-POM

Wrap the yarn several times around a piece of scrap cardboard. Slide the wraps off the cardboard and tie them off in the center. Clip both ends of the tied-off yarn and fluff out the pom-pom. Use the yarn you tied it off with to attach it to the center of the crown of the hat.

FINISHING

Weave in all ends.

Popcorn Beret

SKILL LEVEL

EASY

This is a great project for crocheters who are still mastering the basic stitches. Bobbles are usually made by working several partial stitches together, but in this pattern the subtle bobbly texture is created by mixing single crochets and treble crochets. This is also a good project to learn blocking (see page 99), as it will help smooth out the work and give the finished hat the desired shape.

4
Medium

YARN
Knit Picks Wool of the Andes Worsted (100% wool; 110 yd./100 m; 1.8 oz./50 g), 3 skeins in Victorian

HOOK
U.S. size H-8 (5.0 mm) crochet hook or size needed to obtain gauge

FINISHED MEASUREMENTS
Circumference at band: 19 in. (48 cm)

GAUGE
8 sts and 10 rnds in popcorn pattern = 2 in. (5 cm)

PATTERN

Ch 4; join with a sl st to form a ring.

Round 1: Ch 1, 8 sc in ring; join with a sl st in beg ch.

Round 2: Ch 1, 2 sc in each st around; join with a sl st in beg ch. (16 sts)

Round 3: Ch 1, *tr in next st, 2 sc in next st; rep from * around; join with a sl st in beg ch. (24 sts)

Round 4: Ch 1, *sc in next 2 sts, 2 sc in next st; rep from * around; join with a sl st in beg ch. (30 sts)

Round 5: Ch 1, *sc in next st, tr in next st, sc in next st, 2 sc in next st; rep from * around; join with a sl st in beg ch. (36 sts)

Round 6: Ch 1, *sc in next 4 sts, 2 sc in next st; rep from * around; join with a sl st in beg ch.

Round 7: Ch 1, *[tr in next st, sc in next st] 2 times, tr in next st, 2 sc in next st; rep from * around; join with a sl st in beg ch.

Round 8: Ch 1, *sc in next 6 sts, 2 sc in next st; rep from * around; join with a sl st in beg ch.

Round 9: Ch 1, *[sc in next st, tr in next st] 3 times, sc in next st, [tr, sc] in next st; rep from * around; join with a sl st in beg ch.

Round 10: Ch 1, *sc in next 8 sts, 2 sc in next st; rep from * around; join with a sl st in beg ch.

Round 11: Ch 1, *[tr in next st, sc in next st] 4 times, tr in next st, 2 sc in next st; rep from * around; join with a sl st in beg ch.

Round 12: Ch 1, *sc in next 10 sts, 2 sc in next st; rep from * around; join with a sl st in beg ch.

Round 13: Ch 1, *[sc in next st, tr in next st] 5 times, sc in next st, [tr, sc] in next st; rep from * around; join with a sl st in beg ch.

Round 14: Ch 1, *sc in next 12 sts, 2 sc in next st; rep from * around; join with a sl st in beg ch.

Round 15: Ch 1, *[tr in next st, sc in next st] 6 times, tr in next st, 2 sc in next st; rep from * around; join with a sl st in beg ch.

Round 16: Ch 1, *sc in next 14 sts, 2 sc in next st; rep from * around; join with a sl st in beg ch.

Round 17: Ch 1, *[sc in next st, tr in next st] 7 times, sc in next st, [tr, sc] in next st; rep from * around; join with a sl st in beg ch.

Round 18: Ch 1, *sc in next 16 sts, 2 sc in next st; rep from * around; join with a sl st in beg ch.

Round 19: Ch 1, *[tr in next st, sc in next st] 8 times, tr in next st, 2 sc in next st; rep from * around; join with a sl st in beg ch.

Round 20: Ch 1, *sc in next 18 sts, 2 sc in next st; rep from * around; join with a sl st in beg ch. (160 sts)

Round 21: Ch 1, *sc in next st, tr in next st; rep from * around; join with a sl st in beg ch.

Round 22: Ch 1, sc in each st around join with a sl st in beg ch.

Round 23: Ch 1, *tr in next st, sc in next st; rep from * around; join with a sl st in beg ch.

Round 24: Repeat Round 22.

Round 25: Ch 1, *[sc in next st, tr in next st] 9 times, sc2tog; rep from * around; join with a sl st in beg ch.

Round 26: Ch 1, *sc in next 17 sts, sc2tog; rep from * around; join with a sl st in beg ch.

Round 27: Ch 1, *[tr in next st, sc in next st] 8 times, sc2tog; rep from * around; join with a sl st in beg ch.

Round 28: Ch 1, *sc in next 15 sts, sc2tog; rep from * around; join with a sl st in beg ch.

Round 29: Ch 1, *[sc in next st, tr in next st] 7 times, sc2tog; rep from * around; join with a sl st in beg ch.

Round 30: Ch 1, *sc in next 13 sts, sc2tog; rep from * around; join with a sl st in beg ch.

Round 31: Ch 1, *[tr in next st, sc in next st] 6 times, sc2tog; rep from * around; join with a sl st in beg ch.

Round 32: Ch 1, *sc in next 11 sts, sc2tog; rep from * around; join with a sl st in beg ch.

> Hat brim should fit head snugly at this point; work more or fewer rounds in this manner as needed. You can end on either an even or odd round.

BAND

Round 33: Ch 1, sc in each st around; join with a sl st in beg ch.

Round 34: Ch 1, dc in each st around; join with a sl st in beg ch.

Round 35: Ch 1, sc in each st around; join with a sl st in beg ch.

Rounds 36–37: Repeat Rounds 34–35.

Fasten off.

FINISHING

Weave in ends. Block hat to give it a more defined shape, if desired.

Summer Sorbet Wrap

Made in very light wool yarn, this delicate wrap is warm enough to keep you comfortable on a brisk spring day but not too bulky. This is a great project for trying out a beautiful variegated sock yarn, like the one used here for the colored stripes.

YARN
Red Heart "Heart & Sole" (70% superwash wool, 30% nylon; 213 yd./195 m; 1.8 oz./50 g), 4 skeins in Ivory (A), 3 skeins in Berry Bliss (B)

Super Fine

HOOK
U.S. size C-2 (2.75 mm) crochet hook or size needed to obtain gauge

FINISHED MEASUREMENTS
Length: 64 in.(163 cm); width: 16 in. (41 cm)

GAUGE
Gauge is flexible for this project. Work a small swatch before you start to make sure you are happy with the drape of the fabric.

PATTERN

With A, make a chain slightly longer than 64 in. (163 cm); the number of chs must be a multiple of 10 plus 4.

Row 1: Tr2tog in 4th ch from hook, sk next 4 ch, tr in next ch, ch 4, tr2tog in 4th ch of ch just made, sk next 4 chs of foundation ch, sl st in next ch, *ch 4, tr2tog in 4th ch of ch just made, sk next 4 chs of foundation ch, tr in next ch, ch 4, tr2tog in 4th ch of ch just made, sk next 4 chs of foundation ch, sl st in next ch; rep from * to end of row.

Row 2: Ch 9, turn. Sl st in next tr, *ch 5, tr in next sl st, ch 5, sl st in next tr; rep from * across, ending with ch 5, tr in base of last tr2tog of prev row.

Row 3: Ch 8, turn. Tr2tog in 4th ch from hook; working around the sl st of the prev row, sc in the next tr of row 1; *ch 4, tr2tog in 4th ch, tr in next tr, ch 4, tr2tog in 4th ch, sc in next tr of row 1 (working over sl st of prev row); rep from * across, ending with a tr in the 5th ch of end loop.

Row 4: Ch 1, turn. Sc in 1st tr, ch 5, tr in next sc, *ch 5, sc in next tr, ch 5, tr in next sc; rep from *

across, ending with ch 5, sc in top ch of end loop. Fasten off; do not turn.

Row 5: Join B in 1st sc of row 4, sc in same st as joining, ch 7, sc in next tr, *ch 7, sc in next sc, ch 7, sc in next tr; rep from * across, ending with ch 7, sc in last sc.

Row 6: Ch 10, turn. Sc in 1st ch-sp, *ch 7, sc in next ch-sp; rep from * across, ending with ch 4, tr in last sc.

Row 7: Turn. *Ch 7, sc in next ch-sp; rep from * across, ending with ch 7, sc in 5th ch of end loop.

Row 8: Ch 10, turn. Sc in first ch-sp, *ch 7, sc in next ch-sp; rep from * across, ending with ch 4, tr in tr. Fasten off; turn.

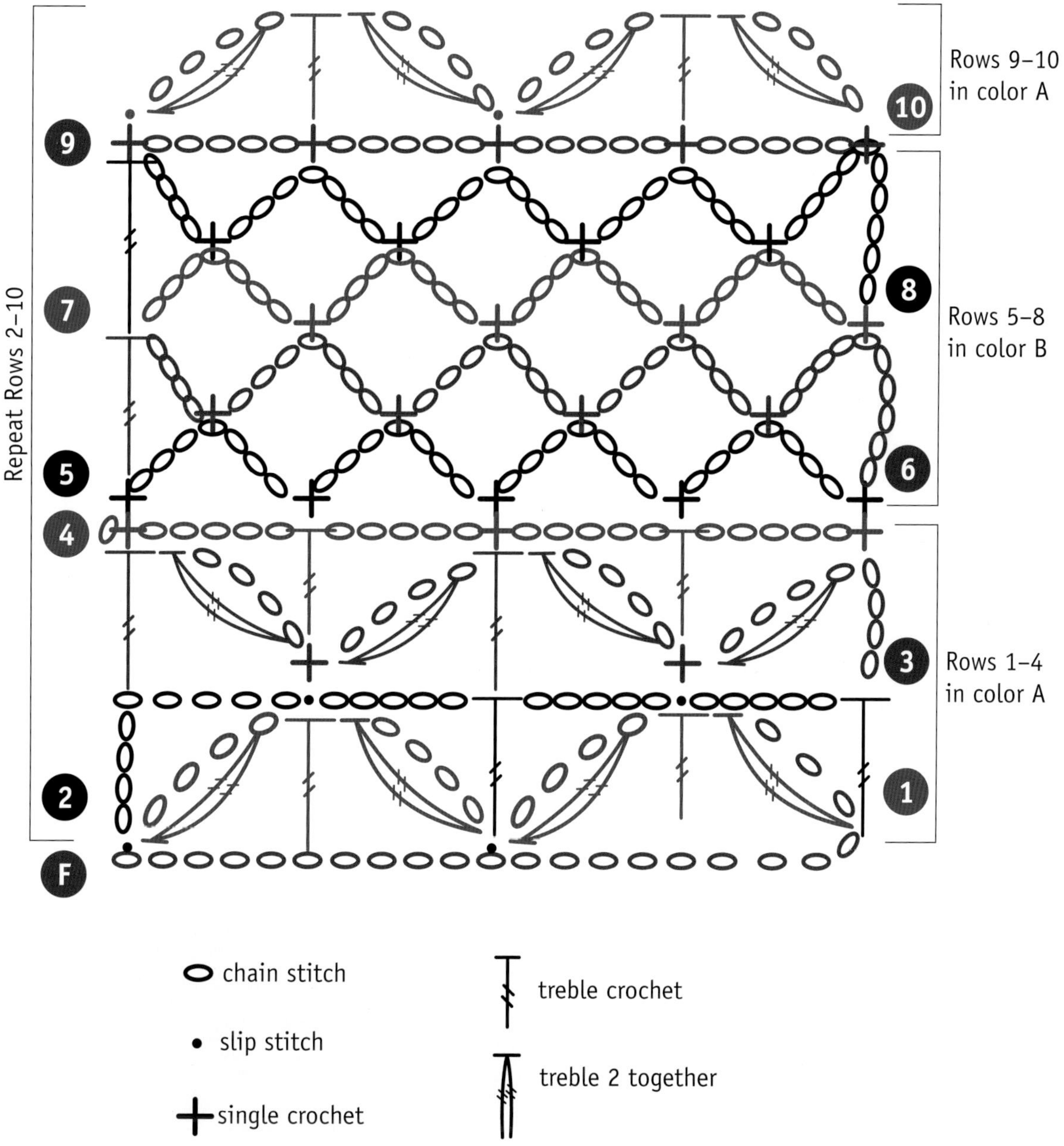

Rows 9–10
in color A

Rows 5–8
in color B

Rows 1–4
in color A

Repeat Rows 2–10

⟲ chain stitch

• slip stitch

✛ single crochet

┬ treble crochet

⟙ treble 2 together

Row 9: Join A in tr just made, sc in same st as joining. *Ch 5, sc in next ch-sp; rep from * across, ending with ch 5, sc in 5th ch of end loop.

Row 10: Turn. *Ch 4, tr2tog in 4th ch, tr in next sc, ch 4, tr2tog in 4th ch, sl st in next sc; rep from * across.

Repeat Rows 2–10 five more times or until wrap is desired width. Finish by working Rows 2–4 once more. Fasten off.

FINISHING

Weave in ends. Block.

The Summer Sorbet Wrap in 1953

Classic Fedora

SKILL LEVEL

INTERMEDIATE

This fedora is crocheted instead of being made from a single piece of felt, but it still looks like it walked right out of a Prohibition-era speakeasy. The only really difficult part of this pattern is placing the tucks at the end; take your time and experiment with them until you're happy with the look.

YARN
Patons Classic Wool (100% wool; 210 yd./192 m; 3.5 oz./ 100 g), 1 skein in Dark Grey Mix

Medium

HOOK
U.S. size F-5 (3.75 mm) crochet hook or size needed to obtain gauge

NOTIONS
Yarn needle
Sewing needle and matching thread

FINISHED MEASUREMENTS
Circumference: 23 in. (58 cm)

GAUGE
4 sts and 4 rnds in sc = 1 in. (2.5 cm)

PATTERN

Ch 4; join with sl st to form a ring.

Round 1: Ch 1, work 7 sc in ring; join with sl st in beg ch.

Round 2: Ch 1, 2 sc in each sc of prev round; join with sl st in beg ch.

Round 3: Ch 1, *2 sc in next st, sc in next st; rep from * around; join with sl st in beg ch.

Round 4: Ch 1, *sc in next 2 sts, 2 sc in next st; rep from * around; join with sl st in beg ch.

Round 5: Ch 1, sc in next st, *2 sc in next st, sc in next 3 sts; rep from * around to last 2 sts, sc in last 2 sts; join with sl st in beg ch.

Round 6: Ch 1, *sc in next 4 sts, 2 sc in next st; rep from * around; join with sl st in beg ch.

Round 7: Ch 1, sc in next 2 sts, *2 sc in next st, sc in next 5 sts; rep from * around to last 3 sts, sc in last 3 sts; join with sl st in beg ch.

Round 8: Ch 1, *sc in next 6 sts, 2 sc in next st; rep from * around; join with sl st in beg ch.

Round 9: Ch 1, sc in next 3 sts, *2 sc in next st, sc in next 7 sts; rep from * around to last 4 sts, sc in last 4 sts; join with sl st in beg ch.

Round 10: Ch 1, *sc in next 8 sts, 2 sc in next st; rep from * around; join with sl st in beg ch.

Round 11: Ch 1, sc in next 4 sts, *2 sc in next st, sc in next 9 sts; rep from * around to last 5 sts, sc in last 5 sts; join with sl st in beg ch.

Round 12: Ch 1, *sc in next 10 sts, 2 sc in next st; rep from * around; join with sl st in beg ch.

Round 13: Ch 1, sc in next 5 sts, *2 sc in next st, sc in next 11 sts; rep from * around to last 6 sts, sc in last 6 sts; join with sl st in beg ch.

At this point, the piece should measure about 6 in. (15 cm) in diameter. The work will proceed in a continuous spiral, without joining at the end of each round. Use a stitch marker or a piece of scrap yarn to mark the first stitch of every round, moving it up to the new round as you complete each round.

Work even in sc in a continuous spiral until work
    measures 7 1/4 in. (18.4 cm) from center to outer
    edge.
Brim Increase Round: *Work 2 sc in next st, sc in
    next st; rep from * around.
Work even in sc until brim measures 2 1/2 in. (6.4 cm)
    from Brim Increase Round.
Last Round: *Sc2tog, sc in next st; rep from *
    around. Sl st in first st of round to even out end
    of round. Fasten off.

FINISHING
Weave in ends.
Turn under a hem 3/4 in. (1.9 cm) deep and sew.
Form two long tucks in the crown of the hat, one
    on each side slanting inward toward the front.
    Working from the inside of the hat, sew the top
of the hat to the side loosely at one or two
places inside each tuck to hold them in place.
Add a smaller tuck straight across the back edge
of the crown and sew it in the same way.
Sew the ribbon around hat along Brim Increase
    Round.

Beaded Handbag

SKILL LEVEL

■■■□

INTERMEDIATE

This sturdy cotton handbag will hold all your essentials without getting stretched out of shape. The lining and zipper help to hold even small objects safely inside. This purse is a great project for trying out crocheting with beads strung onto the yarn; the beads are only used in the trim, which is crocheted separately and sewn on at the end, making the beaded portion very manageable.

3
Light

YARN
Patons Grace (100% mercerized cotton; 136 yd./125 m; 1.75 oz./ 50 g), 4 skeins in Orchid

HOOKS
U.S. size D-3 (3.25 mm) crochet hook or size needed to obtain gauge
U.S. size B-2 (2.25 mm) crochet hook

NOTIONS
48 clear beads, about $3/8$ in. (1 cm) in diameter
Zipper, 11 inches long
$1/4$ yd. cotton fabric for lining
Piece of cardboard
Sewing needle and matching thread

FINISHED MEASUREMENTS
Bottom: 8 by $4^1/2$ in. (20 by 11 cm) oval; height, not counting handles: $8^1/2$ in. (22 cm)

GAUGE
11 sts and 11 rnds in sc with larger hook = 2 in. (5 cm)

PATTERN

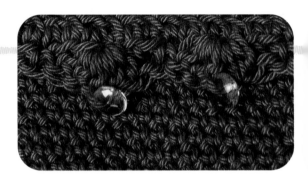

BASE
With larger hook, ch 17.
Round 1: 3 sc in 2nd ch from hook, sc in each ch across to last ch, 3 sc in last ch; turn and continue across the back of the foundation chain, working 1 sc in each ch to end.
Round 2: Sc in each sc around, increasing 3 sts evenly around each rounded end.
Repeat Round 2 until piece measures $8^1/2$ in. (26 cm) long.

SIDE
Round 1: Sc tbl in each st around.
Round 2: Sc in each st around.
Rounds 3–6: Repeat Round 2.
Increase Round: Sc in each st around, increasing 1 st somewhere near the middle of each side of the bag.

Work even in sc for 1 in. (2.5 cm), then repeat the Increase Round, placing the increases at a slightly different point on each side to avoid an obvious increase ridge.
Continue in this pattern until a total of 5 Increase Rounds have been worked.
Work even until side measures 8 in. (20 cm). Sl st in next st.
Next round: Turn, sl st in each st around. Fasten off.

TRIM

Thread the beads onto the yarn. Make a chain long enough to reach loosely around the bag (must be a multiple of 5 + 3).

Row 1: Sc in 2nd ch from hook and in each ch across. Turn.

Row 2: Ch 1, turn. Sc in first st, *sk next 2 sts, in next st work 5 dc, pulling up a bead so that it ends up on top of the 3rd dc, sk next 2 sts, sc in next st; rep from * across.

Fasten off.

Make 3 scalloped strips long enough to go around the bag—one to fit around the top edge, another to fit around 2 in. (5 cm) lower, and the third another 2 in. (5 cm) lower. Sew the strips to the bag.

HANDLE (MAKE 2)

With smaller hook, ch 10. Join with sl st to form a ring.

Round 1: Ch 1, sc in each ch around.

Round 2: Sc in each st around.

Repeat Round 2 until piece measures 14 1/2 in. (36 cm) long. Fasten off.

Sew handles to the top edge of the bag.

FINISHING

Fold the lining fabric in two, then lay it out with the bag on top. Trace around the bag, then cut out along the traced lines, leaving about 1 in. extra on the top edge, to get two pieces the size of the bag. With wrong sides together, sew around the sides and bottom edge of the two pieces.

Turn down to the outside about 1/2 in. (1.3 cm) all the way around the top edge of the lining and press. Turn down another 1/2 in. (1.3 cm) and press again. Sew the zipper to the top edge of the lining. Insert the lining inside the bag and sew it to the bag all the way around the top edge with invisible stitches.

Cut an oval of cardboard about 1/4 in. (0.6 cm) smaller all around than the bottom of the bag. Cut two pieces of lining fabric about 1/2 in. (1.3 cm) larger than the oval on all sides. With wrong sides together, sew around the long sides and one rounded edge of the fabric ovals. Turn right side out and slip the cardboard inside. Hand-stitch the open end of the fabric closed. Place this covered cardboard piece in the bottom of the purse.

Red Apple Beret

This lightweight beret is quick and easy to make, and uses less than a skein of yarn. It has a very pronounced hexagonal structure: If you like it this way, you're all set; if not, a quick blocking evens out the corners and allows you to shape it however you want.

YARN
Knit Picks Swish DK (100% superwash wool; 123 yd./ 112 m; 1.8 oz./50 g), 1 skein in Serrano

FINISHED MEASUREMENTS
Circumference at brim: 18 in. (46 cm)

GAUGE
Circumference of first 4 rounds: 3 in. (8 cm)

HOOKS
U.S. size H-8 (5.0 mm) crochet hook or size needed to obtain gauge
U.S. size G-6 (4.0 mm) crochet hook (or hook 1 mm smaller than main hook)

PATTERN

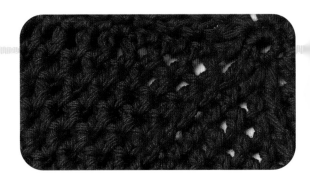

With larger crochet hook, ch 4; join with sl st to form a ring.

Round 1: Ch 1, work 6 sc in ring. Join with sl st in beginning ch.

Round 2: Ch 3, hdc in next st, ch 1, [hdc, ch1] twice in next 5 sts; join with sl st in 2nd ch of beg ch-3.

Round 3: Ch 3 (counts as first hdc, ch 1, throughout), hdc in same ch-sp as joining, ch 1; *FPhdc around next hdc, ch 1, [hdc in next ch-sp, ch 1] twice; rep from * around, FPhdc around last hdc, ch 1, join with sl st in 2nd ch of beg ch-3.

Round 4: Ch 3, hdc in same ch-sp as joining, ch 1, hdc in next ch-sp, ch 1; *FPhdc around next hdc, ch 1, [hdc in next ch-sp, ch 1] 3 times; rep from * around, FPhdc around last hdc, ch 1, join with sl st in 2nd ch of beg ch-3.

Round 5: Ch 3, hdc in same ch-sp as joining, ch 1, [hdc in next ch-sp, ch 1] twice; *FPhdc around next hdc, ch 1, [hdc in next ch-sp, ch 1] 4 times; rep from * around, FPhdc around last hdc, ch 1, join with sl st in 2nd ch of beg ch-3.

Round 6: Ch 3, hdc in same ch-sp as joining, ch 1, [hdc in next ch-sp, ch 1] 3 times; *FPhdc around next hdc, ch 1, [hdc in next ch-sp, ch 1] 5 times; rep from * around, FPhdc around last hdc, ch 1, join with sl st in 2nd ch of beg ch-3.

Round 7: Ch 3, hdc in same ch-sp as joining, ch 1, [hdc in next ch-sp, ch 1] 4 times; *FPhdc around next hdc, ch 1, [hdc in next ch-sp, ch 1] 6 times; rep from * around, FPhdc around last hdc, ch 1, join with sl st in 2nd ch of beg ch-3.

Round 8: Ch 3, hdc in same ch-sp as joining, ch 1, [hdc in next ch-sp, ch 1] 5 times; *FPhdc around next hdc, ch 1, [hdc in next ch-sp, ch 1] 7 times; rep from * around, FPhdc around last hdc, ch 1, join with sl st in 2nd ch of beg ch-3.

Round 9: Ch 3, hdc in same ch-sp as joining, ch 1, [hdc in next ch-sp, ch 1] 6 times; *FPhdc around next hdc, ch 1, [hdc in next ch-sp, ch 1] 8 times; rep from * around, FPhdc around last hdc, ch 1, join with sl st in 2nd ch of beg ch-3.

Round 10: Ch 3, hdc in same ch-sp as joining, ch 1, [hdc in next ch-sp, ch 1] 7 times; *FPhdc around next hdc, ch 1, [hdc in next ch-sp, ch 1] 9 times; rep from * around, FPhdc around last hdc, ch 1, join with sl st in 2nd ch of beg ch-3.

Round 11: Ch 3, hdc in same ch-sp as joining, ch 1, [hdc in next ch-sp, ch 1] 8 times; *FPhdc around next hdc, ch 1, [hdc in next ch-sp, ch 1] 10 times; rep from * around, FPhdc around last hdc, ch 1, join with sl st in 2nd ch of beg ch-3.

Round 12: Ch 3, hdc in same ch-sp as joining, ch 1, [hdc in next ch-sp, ch 1] 9 times; *FPhdc around next hdc, ch 1, [hdc in next ch-sp, ch 1] 11 times; rep from * around, FPhdc around last hdc, ch 1, join with sl st in 2nd ch of beg ch-3.

Round 13: Ch 3, hdc in same ch-sp as joining, ch 1, [hdc in next ch-sp, ch 1] 10 times; *FPhdc around next hdc, ch 1, [hdc in next ch-sp, ch 1] 12 times; rep from * around, FPhdc around last hdc, ch 1, join with sl st in 2nd ch of beg ch-3.

Round 14: Ch 3, hdc in same ch-sp as joining, ch 1, [hdc in next ch-sp, ch 1] 11 times; *FPhdc around next hdc, ch 1, [hdc in next ch-sp, ch 1] 13 times; rep from * around, FPhdc around last hdc, ch 1, join with sl st in 2nd ch of beg ch-3.

Round 15: Ch 3, hdc in same ch-sp as joining, ch 1, [hdc in next ch-sp, ch 1] 12 times; *FPhdc around next hdc, ch 1, [hdc in next ch-sp, ch 1] 14 times; rep from * around, FPhdc around last hdc, ch 1, join with sl st in 2nd ch of beg ch-3.

Round 16: Ch 3, hdc in same ch-sp as joining, ch 1, [hdc in next ch-sp, ch 1] 13 times; *FPhdc around next hdc, ch 1, [hdc in next ch-sp, ch 1] 15 times; rep from * around, FPhdc around last hdc, ch 1, join with sl st in 2nd ch of beg ch-3.

Round 17: Ch 3, skip same ch-sp as joining, [hdc in next ch-sp, ch 1] 13 times; *FPhdc around next hdc, ch 1, skip next ch-sp, [hdc in next ch-sp, ch 1] 14 times, skip next ch-sp; rep from * around, FPhdc around last hdc, ch 1, join with sl st in 2nd ch of beg ch-3.

Round 18: Ch 3, skip same ch-sp as joining, [hdc in next ch-sp, ch 1] 12 times; *FPhdc around next hdc, ch 1, skip next ch-sp, [hdc in next ch-sp, ch 1] 13 times, skip next ch-sp; rep from * around, FPhdc around last hdc, ch 1, join with sl st in 2nd ch of beg ch-3.

Round 19: Ch 3, skip same ch-sp as joining, [hdc in next ch-sp, ch 1] 11 times; *FPhdc around next hdc, ch 1, skip next ch-sp, [hdc in next ch-sp, ch 1] 12 times, skip next ch-sp; rep from * around, FPhdc around last hdc, ch 1, join with sl st in 2nd ch of beg ch-3.

Round 20: Ch 3, skip same ch-sp as joining, [hdc in next ch-sp, ch 1] 10 times; *FPhdc around next hdc, ch 1, skip next ch-sp, [hdc in next ch-sp, ch 1] 12 times, skip next ch-sp; rep from * around, FPhdc around last hdc, ch 1, join with sl st in 2nd ch of beg ch-3.

Round 21: Ch 3, skip same ch-sp as joining, [hdc in next ch-sp, ch 1] 9 times; *FPhdc around next hdc, ch 1, skip next ch-sp, [hdc in next ch-sp, ch 1] 11 times, skip next ch-sp; rep from * around, FPhdc around last hdc, ch 1, join with sl st in 2nd ch of beg ch-3.

Round 22: Ch 3, skip same ch-sp as joining, [hdc in next ch-sp, ch 1] 2 times, hdc2tog over next 2 ch-sps, ch 1, [hdc in next ch-sp, ch 1] 4 times, skip next ch-sp; *FPhdc around next hdc, ch 1, skip next ch-sp, [hdc in next ch-sp, ch 1] 4 times, hdc2tog over next 2 ch-sps, ch 1, [hdc in next ch-sp, ch 1] 4 times, skip next ch-sp; rep from * around, FPhdc around last hdc, ch 1, join with sl st in 2nd ch of beg ch-3.

Round 23: Ch 3, skip same ch-sp as joining, [hdc in next ch-sp, ch 1] 6 times; *FPhdc around next hdc, ch 1, skip next ch-sp, [hdc in next ch-sp, ch 1] 8 times, skip next ch-sp; rep from * around, FPhdc around last hdc, ch 1, join with sl st in 2nd ch of beg ch-3.

Round 24: Ch 3, skip same ch-sp as joining, hdc2tog over next 2 ch-sps, ch 1, hdc in next ch-sp, ch 1, hdc2tog over next 2 ch-sps, ch 1, skip next ch-sp; *FPhdc around next hdc, ch 1, skip next ch-sp, [hdc in next ch-sp, ch 1, hdc2tog over next 2 ch-sps, ch 1] twice, hdc in next ch-sp, ch 1; rep from * around, FPhdc around last hdc, ch 1, join with sl st in 2nd ch of beg ch-3.

Round 25: Ch 1, sc in same ch-sp as joining, *FPsc around next st, sc in next ch-sp; rep from * around, join with sl st in beg ch.

Change to smaller hook.

Round 26: Ch 1, sc in each st around, join with a sl st in beg ch.

Rounds 27–28: Repeat Round 26.

Fasten off.

FINISHING

Weave in ends.

This hat naturally forms a hexagonal shape with fairly prominent corners. If you like this shape, then you're done! If you want a softer, more circular hat, block the project by getting it wet, squeezing out the water (do not wring), and laying the hat out to dry on a folded towel. Shape the hat as you lay it out, softening the corners and evening out the edge; it will retain the shape when it dries.

Flower Child Hat and Purse

With this hat and purse set, your little one will carry spring with her, even on the grayest, drizzly day! The simple cloche-style hat and the matching bag are worked entirely in single crochet, creating a green field that you can speckle with flowers in all different sizes and spring colors.

Super Fine

YARN
Knit Picks Comfy Fingering (75% pima cotton, 25% acrylic; 218 yd./200 m; 1.8 oz./50 g), 3 skeins in Peapod, 1 skein each in Flamingo, Sea Foam, Lilac Mist, Seminola, and White

Amounts given are enough to make both the hat and the bag.

HOOK
U.S. size E-4 (3.5 mm) crochet hook or size needed to obtain gauge

NOTION
Yarn needle

FINISHED MEASUREMENTS
Circumference: 21 in. (53 cm)

GAUGE
6 sts and 6.5 rnds in sc = 1 in. (2.5 cm)

The hat and bag are worked in continuous rounds; mark the end of each round but do not join at the ends of rounds.

HAT

Ch 4, join with sl st to form a ring.
Round 1: 6 sc in ring.
Round 2: Work 2 sc in each st around.
Round 3: *Sc in next st, 2 sc in next st; rep from * around.
Round 4: *Sc in next 2 sts, 2 sc in next st; rep from * around.
Round 5: *Sc in next st, 2 sc in next st, sc in next 2 sts; rep from * around.
Round 6: *Sc in next 4 sts, 2 sc in next st; rep from * around.
Round 7: *Sc in next st, 2 sc in next st, sc in next 4 sts; rep from * around.
Round 8: *Sc in next 4 sts, 2 sc in next st, sc in next 2 sts; rep from * around.
Round 9: *2 sc in next st, sc in next 7 sts; rep from * around.
Round 10: *Sc in next 7 sts, 2 sc in next st, sc in next st; rep from * around.

Round 11: *Sc in next 3 sts, 2 sc in next st, sc in next 6 sts; rep from * around.
Round 12: *Sc in next 10 sts, 2 sc in next st; rep from * around.
Round 13: *Sc in next 6 sts, 2 sc in next st, sc in next 5 sts; rep from * around.
Round 14: *Sc in next st, 2 sc in next st, sc in next 11 sts; rep from * around.
Round 15: *Sc in next 10 sts, 2 sc in next st, sc in next 3 sts; rep from * around.
Round 16: *Sc in next 4 sts, 2 sc in next st, sc in next 10 sts; rep from * around.

Round 17: *Sc in next 15 sts, 2 sc in next st; rep from * around.

Round 18: *Sc in next 3 sts, 2 sc in next st, sc in next 13 sts; rep from * around.

Round 19: *Sc in next 11 sts, 2 sc in next st, sc in next 6 sts; rep from * around.

Round 20: Sc in each st around.

Repeat Round 20 until piece measures 5³⁄₄ in. (14.6 cm) from the center of the crown to the edge (or desired length to fit head).

BRIM

Round 1: *Sc in next 6 sts, 2 sc in next st; rep from * to last 2 sts, sc in last 2 sts.

Round 2: Sc in each st around.

Rounds 3–12: Repeat Round 2.

Fasten off.

Turn under last 3 rounds of brim and sew to inside of hat.

FLOWERS

Three different flower patterns are given here. Make as many as you like in whatever sizes and colors you prefer. Hat pictured shows 32 flowers.

Large Flower

Ch 4, join with a sl st to form a ring.

Round 1: *Ch 3, tr twice in ring, ch 3, sl st in ring; rep from * 4 more times; join with sl st in 1st ch of beg ch-3. Fasten off.

Medium Flower

Ch 4, join with a sl st to form a ring.

Round 1: *Ch 3, dc twice in ring, ch 3, sl st in ring; rep from * 4 more times; join with sl st in 1st ch of beg ch-3. Fasten off.

Small Flower

Ch 4, join with a sl st to form a ring.

Round 1: *Ch 2, dc in ring, ch 2, sl st in ring; rep from * 5 more times; join with sl st in 1st ch of beg ch-2. Fasten off.

FINISHING

Sew flowers along brim of hat. Weave in ends.

PURSE

Ch 28.

Round 1: 3 sc in second ch from hook, work 1 sc in each ch to last ch, 3 sc in last ch; working across the back of the chain, work 1 sc in each ch; place marker for end of round.

Round 2: 2 sc in each of next 3 sts, sc in next 25 sts, 2 sc in each of next 3 sts, sc in each st to end of round.

Round 3: *[2 sc in next st, sc in next st] 3 times, sc in next 25 sts; rep from * once.

Round 4: *[sc in next 2 sts, 2 sc in next st] 3 times, sc in next 25 sts; rep from * once.

Round 5: *[2 sc in next st, sc in next 3 sts] 3 times, sc in next 25 sts; rep from * once.

Round 6: *[sc in next 3 sts, 2 sc in next st, sc in next st] 3 times, sc in next 25 sts; rep from * once.

Round 7: *[sc in next st, 2 sc in next st, sc in next 4 sts] 3 times, sc in next 25 sts; rep from * once.

Round 8: *[sc in next 6 sts, 2 sc in next st] 3 times, sc in next 25 sts; rep from * once.

Round 9: *[sc in next 3 sts, 2 sc in next st, sc in next 4 sts] 3 times, sc in next 25 sts; rep from * once.

Round 10: Sc tbl in each st around.

Round 11: Sc in each st around (through both loops).

Repeat Round 11 until bag measures 7 1/2 in. (19 cm) from Round 10.

Sl st in next 2 sts to even out top edge, then fasten off.

Turn down 1 1/2 in. (3.8 cm) around top edge of bag and sew to inside.

HANDLE (MAKE 2)

Ch 45.

Row 1: Sc in second ch from hook and in each ch across. Ch 1, turn.

Row 2: Sc in each st across; ch 1, turn.

Rows 3–4: Repeat Row 2.

Fasten off.

Fold piece lengthwise and sew long edges together to form a tube.

FLOWERS

Following the patterns given in the hat pattern, make 24 flowers in various colors.

FINISHING

Sew the handles to the inside top edge of the bag on each side. Sew the flowers around the top edge. Weave in ends.

Resources

Don't feel too bound by skill levels. There is a lot of variation within a skill level, so a pattern that is classified as Easy could be only a little more difficult than a Beginner pattern—or it might be almost an Intermediate pattern. If there's a pattern you like that is a higher skill level than you have done before, give it a try anyway; take it slow, study the photo of the finished item carefully, look up tutorials for any stitches you don't know, and you'll be fine!

The chart below gives a broad outline of the kinds of skills and techniques you can expect in a project of each skill level.

All the yarn recommendations in this book are given using the Standard Yarn Weight System developed by the Craft Yarn Council of America. This system is a way of sorting yarn by weight, or thickness, and can be helpful in finding an appropriate substitute if you can't find or don't want to use the yarn given in a pattern. Be aware that two yarns in the same category are not always interchangeable. To make sure the yarn you want to use will work for the project you have in mind, check the gauge before you start.

SKILL LEVELS FOR CROCHET

1 ◨☐☐☐ **Beginner**	Projects for first-time crocheters using basic stitches. Minimal shaping.	
2 ◨■☐☐ **Easy**	Projects with basic stitches, repetitive stitch patterns, simple color changes, and simple shaping and finishing.	
3 ◨■■☐ **Intermediate**	Projects using a variety of techniques, such as basic lace patterns or color patterns, mid-level shaping and finishing.	
4 ◨■■◧ **Experienced**	Projects with intricate stitch patterns, techniques and dimension, such as non-repeating patterns, multicolor techniques, fine threads, small hooks, detailed shaping and refined finishing.	

This Standards & Guidelines booklet and downloadable symbol artwork are available at: **YarnStandards.com**

Source: Craft Yarn Council of America's www.YarnStandards.com

STANDARDS & GUIDELINES FOR CROCHET AND KNITTING

Standard Yarn Weight System

Categories of yarn, gauge ranges, and recommended needle and hook sizes

Yarn Weight Symbol & Category Names	0 Lace	1 Super Fine	2 Fine	3 Light	4 Medium	5 Bulky	6 Super Bulky
Type of Yarns in Category	Fingering 10 count crochet thread	Sock, Fingering, Baby	Sport, Baby	DK, Light Worsted	Worsted, Afghan, Aran	Chunky, Craft, Rug	Bulky, Roving
Knit Gauge Range* in Stockinette Stitch to 4 inches	33–40** sts	27–32 sts	23–26 sts	21–24 sts	16–20 sts	12–15 sts	6–11 sts
Recommended Needle in Metric Size Range	1.5–2.25 mm	2.25–3.25 mm	3.25–3.75 mm	3.75–4.5 mm	4.5–5.5 mm	5.5–8 mm	8 mm and larger
Recommended Needle U.S. Size Range	000 to 1	1 to 3	3 to 5	5 to 7	7 to 9	9 to 11	11 and larger
Crochet Gauge* Ranges in Single Crochet to 4 inch	32-42 double crochets**	21–32 sts	16–20 sts	12–17 sts	11–14 sts	8–11 sts	5–9 sts
Recommended Hook in Metric Size Range	Steel*** 1.6–1.4mm Regular hook 2.25 mm	2.25–3.5 mm	3.5–4.5 mm	4.5–5.5 mm	5.5–6.5 mm	6.5–9 mm	9 mm and larger
Recommended Hook U.S. Size Range	Steel*** 6, 7, 8 Regular hook B–1	B–1 to E–4	E–4 to 7	7 to I–9	I–9 to K–10½	K–10½ to M–13	M–13 and larger

* GUIDELINES ONLY: The above reflect the most commonly used gauges and needle or hook sizes for specific yarn categories.

** Lace weight yarns are usually knitted or crocheted on larger needles and hooks to create lacy, openwork patterns. Accordingly, a gauge range is difficult to determine. Always follow the gauge stated in your pattern.

*** Steel crochet hooks are sized differently from regular hooks--the higher the number, the smaller the hook, which is the reverse of regular hook sizing.

This Standards & Guidelines booklet and downloadable symbol artwork are available at: **YarnStandards.com**

Source: Craft Yarn Council of America's www.YarnStandards.com

GAUGE

To save time, check your gauge. Working up a gauge swatch only to have to pull it out again so you can start the actual pattern may seem like a waste of time, but it is an essential step for any project that needs to be a specific size. Even with projects that don't need to be a particular size, such as a tote bag or a shawl, it is still a good idea to crochet a test swatch to make sure you like the fabric that is produced with the hook and yarn combination you have chosen. Changing your mind after 8 rows worked over 10 stitches is a lot less painful than changing your mind after 8 rows of 150 stitches!

How to check your gauge. A gauge swatch is really just a small section of a pattern. Sometimes a pattern will tell you exactly what to crochet for a gauge swatch (e.g., "the first 4 rounds of the base of the bag"); if not, just make a chain several stitches longer than the number of stitches mentioned in the gauge information. For example, if the gauge information reads "8 sts and 9 rnds in sc = 2 in. (5 cm)" you might start with a foundation chain of 12 to 16 chains. Work in even rows of whatever stitch is indicated in the gauge information (in our example, single crochet; if the gauge information says "in pattern" look to the main part of the pattern to find the instructions for the basic stitch pattern used most in the project) until the swatch is a bit taller than the measurement given (in our example, work until the piece measures 3 in. [7.5 cm]).

Once you have your swatch, lay it out, measure out the width and height given, and count how many stitches you have within those measurements. If you have more stitches or rows than given in the gauge information (perhaps 12 stitches in 2 in. [5cm]), you are working more tightly than the person who developed the pattern and made the example shown; try using a larger hook (or possibly a thicker yarn). If you have fewer stitches or rows (6 rows in 2 in. [5 cm]), you are working more loosely and should try a smaller hook or lighter-weight yarn. If you decide to change your hook or yarn, *check your gauge again.* It's not easy to predict how much of a difference changing your hook size will make. Taking the time to check your gauge will help you get a finished project in the size you want.

BLOCKING

Blocking is an important step in finishing many projects. It has a huge effect on the final look of a piece, evening out little inconsistencies in your work and allowing you to shape the article into the shape or fit you want. To block a crocheted piece, wet it thoroughly (this loosens up the yarn fibers), then gently squeeze out as much water as you can without wringing the fabric. Lay the damp item out on a towel or other protected surface and use your fingers to gently shape it. (If the project is slightly too large or too small, you can gently stretch or compress it at this stage.) For lace shawls and other garments with small crocheted points you may need to pin parts of the project to the towel to hold them where you want them until they dry (be sure to use rust-proof pins), but for most hats, bags, and so on, pins aren't necessary. When the project dries, it will hold the approximate shape you formed it into and will have a much smoother, more professional finished look.

Abbreviations

The following abbreviations are used throughout the book. Special sitches or abbreviations used in just one pattern are defined in the pattern notes.

beg	beginning
BP	back post
BPsc	back post single crochet
CC	contrasting color
ch	chain
ch-n	section of n chains (e.g., "sl st in top of beg ch-3")
ch-sp	chain space (of 1 ch)
ch-2 sp	chain-2 space
dc	double crochet
dc2tog	double crochet 2 together
FL	front loop(s)
FP	front post
FPdc	front post double crochet
FPsc	front post single crochet
hdc	half double crochet
MC	main color
prev	previous
rep	repeat
rnd(s)	round(s)
RS	right side
sc	single crochet
sc2tog	single crochet 2 together
sk	skip
sl st	slip stitch
sp(s)	space(s)
st(s)	stitch(es)
tbl	through the back loop
tfl	through the front loop
tog	together
tr	treble crochet
WS	wrong side

Visual Index

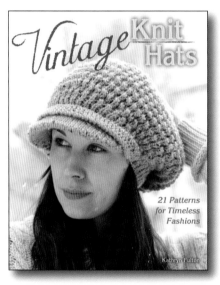
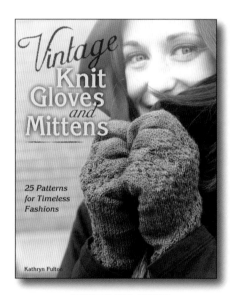